THE GOLDEN ASS

Peter Oswald

THE GOLDEN ASS

or

THE CURIOUS MAN

from the novel by
Lucius Apuleius

OBERON BOOKS
LONDON

First published in 2002 by Oberon Books Ltd.
(incorporating Absolute Classics)
521 Caledonian Road, London N7 9RH
Tel: 020 7607 3637 / Fax: 020 7607 3629
e-mail: oberon.books@btinternet.com

A catalogue record for this book is available from the British
Library.

ISBN: 1 84002 285 X

Cover typography: GTF

Printed in Great Britain by Antony Rowe Ltd, Chippenham.

Characters

PART TWO

LUCIUS, now an ass

ROBARTES, a robber

DECIUS, a robber

HYPOTROPHUS, a robber

OLD WOMAN

HOSTUS

SEXTUS

BALBUS

HORSE

LAMATHUS

ALEXANDROS

CHARITE

TLEPOLEMUS

VENUS

CUPID

PYTHIA

PSYCHE

Her TWO SISTERS

RIVER

ANTS

An EAGLE

A TOWER

JUPITER

GROOM

MARES

STALLIONS

PART THREE

LUCIUS, still an ass
RINGMASTER
THIASUS
SLAVES
SESTOS, a shepherd
ABYDOS, a shepherd
BEAR
MOTHER
RAPSIOS
CHARITE
THRASILLUS
TLEPOLEMUS
STATUE
AUCTIONEER
BAKER
WIFE
FRIEND
LOVER
WIFE OF HONORIUS
YOUNG MAN
HONORIUS
Two STORIES
MELLITUS
CLYTUS
ARISTOMENUS
MASSIMA
HERALD
LIONS
ISIS
PRIEST

The Golden Ass was first performed at Shakespeare's Globe Theatre on 3 August 2002, with the following cast:

ISIS / PAMPHALE / MASSIMA, Geraldine Alexander

OLD WOMAN, Liam Brennan

PROSTITUTE / BAKER'S WIFE, Michael Brown

PHOTIS, Louise Bush

ROBARTES / TIMINOS' MOTHER, Keith Dunphy

CAPTAIN / JUPITER / HONORIUS' WIFE, Peter Hamilton Dyer

DECIUS / GROOM, Ryan Early

BELLEPHERON / THRASILLUS, Paul Higgins

CLYTUS, Colin Hurley

TOWER / LOVER, Simon Hyde

TLEPOLEMUS / COOK, Richard Katz

Lucius' HORSE / PYTHIA / LOVER, Jan Knightley

ROBBER / TIMINOS, Patrick Lennox

APPOLONIUS / ALEXANDROS / PRIEST, Gary Lilburn

WITCH / WIDOW / SISTER OF PSYCHE / FRIEND OF BAKER'S WIFE, Rhys Meredith

SERVANT TO BYRRHENA / BALBUS, Aled Pugh

MILO / THIASUS / BEAR, John Ramm

LUCIUS, Mark Rylance

ARISTOMENUS / HONORIUS, Peter Shorey

CHARITE, Philippa Stanton

JUDGE / RIVER / BAKER, Bill Stewart

OFFICER / SEXTOS / GROOM, Simon Trinder

OFFICER / HOSTUS, Paul Trussell

SISTER OF PSYCHE / RINGMASTER, Timothy Walker

BYRRHENA / HYPOTROPHUS, Jem Wall

SOCRATES / EAGLE / AUCTIONEER, Albie Woodington

Other parts played by members of the company

Musicians, Dave Berry, Richard Halliday, Phil Hopkins, Gillian McDonagh, Andy Keenan, Dai Pritchard, Irita Kutchmy, Tom Lees, Tom Hammond, Kevin Morgan, Dave Powell, Nick Perry, Neil Rowland, Dave Tosh, Frazer Tannock, Martin Evans, Adrian Woodward, Paul Sharp

Singers

PSYCHE, Amy Freston (Pamela Hay on 8, 9 August and 7, 8 September)

CUPID, James Oxley

Master of Play, Tim Carroll

Master of Design, Laura Hopkins

Master of Music and Composer, Claire Van Kampen

Master of Dance, Siân Williams

Note

The following script was correct at the time of going to press but may differ slightly from the play as performed.

PART ONE

Enter ISIS.

ISIS: Now let me tell you an old joke I know
    That happened far away and long ago;
    There was a man who loved a lively lass,
    And for his lust was turned into an ass;
    He suffered many bludgeonings and then
    After some scrapes he was turned back again.
    And most of all I must say this to you:
    This is no joke, it's absolutely true!

Enter LUCIUS riding his horse, which is worn out.

LUCIUS: Easy, my beauty! You have done me proud,
    Over the mountains into the beyond,
    Sliding down scree-slopes, then through plodding fields,
    Clogging and dragging; Holy Thessally,
    The country of my mother's family!
    On his white horse, the unknown son arrives!
    Animal, are you happy? So am I!

Enter ARISTOMENUS and CLYTUS.

CLYTUS: Oh come on!

ARISTOMENUS: I'm telling you!

CLYTUS: Oh leave off, for Christ's sake!

ARISTOMENUS: Straight up!

CLYTUS: I have never, in all my born days –

ARISTOMENUS: Gospel!

CLYTUS: Heard such a stream of tosh gush from a man's mouth.

ARISTOMENUS: You think I could make that up?

CLYTUS: Never has it been my fate to stand downwind of
   such a heap of horseshit.

ARISTOMENUS: Look –

CLYTUS: To be crushed by such a trumpeting herd of
   bollocks.

ARISTOMENUS: You're wrong, Clytus –

CLYTUS: Arrant bollocks, palpable, gross, overblown,
   fatuous balderdash!

ARISTOMENUS: Plain truth –

CLYTUS: What do you take me for?

ARISTOMENUS: Clytus, these things happen.

CLYTUS: They do not.

ARISTOMENUS: They do.

CLYTUS: They do not.

ARISTOMENUS: They do! They did!

LUCIUS: Friends, if I slide into your company,
   Would that enrage you more, or might my ears,
   Wedging themselves between your confrontation,
   Make peace between you by their arbitration?

CLYTUS: It's sick, the whole business, you should padlock
   your fantasies, Aristomenus, otherwise frustrated
   flexisexual suits up from Athens start thinking that in
   Thesally you can get anything you want by magic!

ARISTOMENUS: You can!

LUCIUS: What is the substance of your argument?

CLYTUS: (*Replying to ARISTOMENUS.*) Well yes – that
   encourages the locals to GIVE them whatever they want!
   It's a vicious circle, spun by the hand of the
   pornographic imagination.

LUCIUS: What does he not believe? Tell me, my friend,
    I will believe it, I am not a cynic.

CLYTUS: People want to get drunk, they invent wine;
    people want to kill each other, they invent war; people
    want magic, and they invent superstitions and witches
    and that's what we've got in this country! We're up to our
    necks in it – and we asked for it!

ARISTOMENUS: Well I can only say what happened to
    me!

LUCIUS: I cannot let this pass! I am a man
    Addicted to all curiosities –
    In fact, I think it is the oddities
    Of life, the quirks of fate, the puzzling signs,
    The slips, exceptions and monstrosities,
    That can explain the rest, they form the key
    To the whole code! How on earth else can heaven
    Get our attention? I have come from Athens,
    Where reason reigns, but even there things happen –
    As I was leaving I saw something strange
    Beside the Painted Gate; a juggler swallowed
    A spear, then drew it smoothly out behind,
    Without a grimace – then he held it up,
    And at the top a little boy appeared,
    Who writhed like ivy round the shaft! Good Lord,
    I find it hard to swallow lumps of cheese,
    Never mind spears, but I believed my eyes!
    I am a man of no experience,
    But I am gifted with an open mind –

CLYTUS: First time in the north?

LUCIUS: Indeed it is. My name is Lucius.
    To lift us up the steepness of this hill,
    Friend, can we listen to your story now?

CLYTUS: Oh please!

ARISTOMENUS: Listen, this man does not know Thesally.
    To learn the kind of place to which he's come
    All sharp and shaven from debating Athens,
    Could save his life!

LUCIUS: My life is in your hands.

ARISTOMENUS: Travelling from Aegina, selling cheese,
    I bumped into my old friend Socrates.
    Not the philosopher.

Enter SOCRATES in rags, who's sits down begging.

SOCRATES: Sorry for asking – could you spare some
    change?

ARISTOMENUS: Socrates?

SOCRATES: Yes?

ARISTOMENUS: It's Aristomenus!
    What happened to you?

SOCRATES: Horror! Terror! Murder!
    As I returned from Macedonia,
    Having sold all my pots, a band of robbers
    Beat me and left me bleeding; luckily
    An old but charming woman took me in,
    And I became her lover.

CLYTUS: This is where it starts getting disgusting.

LUCIUS: How old?

SOCRATES: Quite old. But absolutely charming!

ARISTOMENUS:
    You deserve worse than this, you stinking slum!
    To leave your wife, your children and your home
    For an old sagging itchy dribbling granny!

SOCRATES: She is a witch! Be careful what you say!

CLYTUS: Bollocks.

SOCRATES: That is why I have run away from her!

ARISTOMENUS: I took him to the baths – he needed one –
Gave him a meal, and let him share my room.

SOCRATES: I hope my lover does not find us here.
Another man who left her, she turned him into a beaver.
When they're being hunted, they bite off their own balls
and fling them to the dogs to slow them down. That's
how she got her revenge. (*Falls asleep on bed.*)

ARISTOMENUS:
Spirits of light and powers of good stand round
This small hotel, that is so vulnerable
To the big darkness! I will bolt the door
And wedge this chair against it, and this table.
Now I can sleep perhaps. I hear the toll –
One two three four five six seven eight nine ten –

He falls asleep as the last two strikes of midnight chime.

Door bursts open, knocking his bed over and him under it.

Enter MEROE, with sponge and sword.

MEROE: Where is my naughty little boy?
How could you leave your little weasel?
I saved you from the street, and loved you!

*MEROE approaches SOCRATES. She stabs him in the neck
and catches his blood in a pot. She reaches in, feeling about
for his heart.*

Where is his bloody heart? Can't find it!
I should have known he didn't have one!

She drags out various organs.

No that's not it – nor that – nor that –

Finds heart at last and holds it up.

Who wants this bullfrog?

She places the sponge in the wound.

> Faithful sponge,
> When you have served this purpose, be
> Released, and seek your womb the sea!
> Another victory for women!

Exit MEROE.

CLYTUS: No more!

LUCIUS: Go on, I beg you, do not pause!

Sound of guests, woken up by the noise, beating on the door.

ARISTOMENUS: Socrates? Dead! And no one will believe
I did not do it! Save me from the law,
Merciful cord, my plea would not be heard!

Fixes a cord to a beam, and nooses the cord round his neck. Stands on the bed. Cord breaks – he falls on top of SOCRATES, who wakes.

SOCRATES: What are you doing, Aristomenus?
Leave me alone!

ARISTOMENUS: Are you alive, old friend?
Thank heaven! It was all a cheese-based dream!

Noise outside dies away.

SOCRATES: I am alive. But what a hag-riding
I have had too – that feta fries your brains!
Let us get going.

They leave the hotel and come to a stream.

ARISTOMENUS: We had not gone far, when –
Friend, you look pale. Let us sit down, at ease,
Between these streams, and have a bit of cheese.
It is not late, we will not get bad dreams
From this!

SOCRATES: Unless we choose to snooze all day!

They eat cheese.

This cheese is dry, it clogs my throat like clay.
I need a drink.

ARISTOMENUS: You have a choice of streams!
And then he bent down to drink, and the sponge flew out
of his neck and he was dead!

*SOCRATES drinks, the sponge flies out of his neck and he
dies.*

No!

ARISTOMENUS screams insanely.

Beware this place, after a few days here,
You will not recognise yourself! Beware!

CLYTUS: Never in the history of gibberish has a naked lie
been so skimpily bikini'd and stretched out on the beach
of incredulity. I see what you're hiding! Farewell!
Murder this idiot. (*Exit.*)

LUCIUS: Friend, I believe your story absolutely.

ARISTOMENUS: No use – no use – (*Exit.*)

Enter OLD WOMAN selling ice creams.

OLD WOMAN: Ices! Ices!
Welcome to Hypata!

LUCIUS: Am I really here?
Well done old horse.

OLD WOMAN: How can I help you, sir?

LUCIUS: I want a girl more lovely than the moon,
I want more gold than any man has seen,
And lastly, this: I want to know all things.

OLD WOMAN: Do you want a flake with that?

LUCIUS: Tell me how I may find the house of Milo!

OLD WOMAN:
Milo? Turn round and walk straight forwards, sir;
He lives beside the city gate, his mansion
Is the collapsing shack that clings in terror
To the old wall. There is a sweet girl there,
Much easier to talk to than the moon,
You could try her. And all the hollowed walls
Are stuffed with gold, but Milo isn't giving.
And his wife knows a thing or two – ask her –
Though what she knows is better left unlearned.
You'd best get on with your adventure then.

LUCIUS: Thank you, I will. Fantastic Hypata!

OLD WOMAN: You will be good though, won't you
Lucius?

Exit OLD WOMAN.

LUCIUS knocks at MILO's door.

PHOTIS: (*Within.*) We're skint! There isn't any money here,
The house is clean, it's like Antarctica,
No gleam of filthy silver anywhere –
Unless you want to borrow?

LUCIUS: I have come
From Athens, I am Lucius – this letter –

He hands over a letter.

PHOTIS consults with MILO, who reads the letter.

This is the place where I will find my way
Up the next step! Forgive me if I seem
Overexcited by arriving here,
But my beloved mother has just died,
Setting me free; I have been far too long
Trapped in the narrow plough-lines of the plains!
These mountains point my heart straight up to heaven.

PHOTIS: Sorry.

LUCIUS: About what?

PHOTIS: Your mum.

LUCIUS: Oh was I talking out loud? I am sorry.

PHOTIS: That's alright, come in!

Enter LUCIUS to MILO and PAMPHALE sitting at supper, PHOTIS serving.

PAMPHALE almost never speaks, but keeps an unerring fixed smile.

MILO: Lucius, welcome, sit down! Pamphale, give up your
    seat for our friend!

LUCIUS: Lady, I beg you, do not move for me!

MILO: Dear friend, I see you are a wealthy man,
    And so indeed our mutual friend implies,
    But we poor folk are not so rich in stools,
    So multiple in sofas and settees,
    So overloaded with ingenious
    Forms of support, that we can all sit down
    At the same time, when suddenly there comes
    Out of the blue, a welcome guest. My friend,
    The less than little that we have is yours.
    You must be tired. Why not lie down?

LUCIUS: I will.
    I am as happy as a man can be.
    Hypata is a town out of a story.

MILO: It is the place we live in, actually.

PAMPHALE: There will be rain tomorrow.

MILO: Oh my God!

LUCIUS: How can you tell?

PAMPHALE: The candle.

MILO: Obviously.

LUCIUS: That should not be surprising – this small flame
　　　Is the sun's son; it is a flickering
　　　And fallen fleck of his sight-giving eye
　　　That oversees the phases of the sky.

He seems about to go on at length.

MILO blows out the candle.

MILO: Good night!

LUCIUS: 　　　　　　Good night! And thank you heartily.

Exeunt – LUCIUS to his room.

　　　How can I lie down? Night is not the time
　　　For sleeping, when the owls are in the sky,
　　　When people turn their secret selves outside,
　　　And mine, too long imprisoned, longs to swoop
　　　Out of the moon and seize a squealing creature!
　　　I think I might have made a good impression
　　　On my hostess. And I could not help noting
　　　The servant thing that would not meet my eyes;
　　　Her hair was shining and it brushed my hand
　　　Like fire – but I am keeling over – damn –
　　　Starving! Well then – tomorrow everything!

He lies down and sleeps.

Dawn breaks. Cock crow. Enter TRADERS to market place.

FIRST TRADER: Mice! Mice! Rabbits!

SECOND TRADER: Spanish courgettes!

THIRD TRADER: Crystals! Crystals!

FIRST TRADER: Mice! Rabbits! Mice!

FOURTH TRADER: Bread!

FIFTH TRADER: Italian rice!

THIRD TRADER: Courgettes!

SIXTH TRADER: Incense!

THIRD TRADER: Courgettes!

FIFTH TRADER: Italian rice!

FIRST TRADER: Parrots! Snakes! Lizards!

SEVENTH TRADER: Japanese seaweed!

THIRD TRADER: Skulls!

FIRST TRADER: Crocodiles!

FOURTH TRADER: Bread!

SEVENTH TRADER: Moroccan biscuits!

THIRD TRADER: Tarot cards! Bones!

SIXTH TRADER: Self-respect!

SEVENTH TRADER: Wisdom! Truth!

PROSTITUTE: Sex!

SIXTH TRADER: Sympathy! Advice! Kindness!

SEVENTH TRADER: Love! Love! Love!

FIRST TRADER: Terrapins!

Enter LUCIUS.

LUCIUS: Eyes cannot see the things of Hypata –
    It is all hidden! What the ears can hear
    Is a mere speck of what is being spoken
    By the old stones! I woke amazed at dawn,
    Sprang from my plank bed! Stumbling through the town,
    Too slow, I reached the gods just as they turned
    Back into statues – but I saw vague figures
    Rise in a blaze of wings to fall as fountains;
    How can I find the crack through which these phantoms
    Have vanished, so that I can see them, hold them!

Enter BYRRHENA and SERVANTS and LADIES.

OLD SERVANT: Lucius?

LUCIUS: Yes?

OLD SERVANT: God help us! Lucius!

BYRRHENA: Lucius? No it can't be!

OLD SERVANT: Lucius?

LUCIUS: As I said – yes?

BYRRHENA: It is my sister's face.
    You have your mother's beauty, Lucius!
    Lucius, it is truly Lucius!
    Come to my arms!

LUCIUS: You are extremely gracious –

OLD SERVANT: It is your aunt Byrrhena, Lucius!
    Kiss her! Go on!

LUCIUS: This is a public place.

BYRRHENA: In Hypata relations may embrace!

    They kiss.

    I brought you up till you were four! What grace
    Has led you out of Athens to my house?
    Oh now I see my sister is not dead –
    This is the way she stood, not stiff but straight,
    With her chin sticking forwards, obdurate
    But not unpleasant! And her slenderness
    Is copied in your form, not yet filled out
    Too much! You have her rustic ruddiness,
    And her fine hair – though not so much of it!
    Stay at my house, dear heart, let me replace
    Your much-missed mother! Why did you not write
    To tell me you were coming, my sweet light?

LUCIUS: I thank you for your invitation, aunt,
    But it would not be courteous to my host,
    Milo, for me to seek another roost,
    No matter how attractive. May I call,
    Whenever I am passing, at your house,
    And see how you are doing?

BYRRHENA: This is it!
    Call now!

LUCIUS: Dear aunt, this is a fairy palace,
    Wonderful sculptures! They are more alive
    Than you and I, though we have eyes to look,
    And they have eyes only for looking at!

BYRRHENA: Brilliant!

LUCIUS: What is this scene?

BYRRHENA: The hunter is Actaeon;
    These are his hounds. They have been following
    The scent of something not of our dimension,
    Diana, goddess of the hunt, here bathing
    In a bright spring. Actaeon, hurrying
    To where his dogs are crying, sees her shining
    Like a new sun. His own pack turns on him,
    And he is torn to pieces…did you say
    That you are lodging at the house of Milo?

LUCIUS: His friend Demeas sent me there.

BYRRHENA: Be careful!
    The mistress of the house is not a lady.

LUCIUS: What do you mean?

BYRRHENA: Beware of Pamphale!
    She is a first-rate witch, which is to say
    She has a hunger for young men, requiring
    Terrible spells to keep her door revolving.
    Try to be ugly when she looks at you,
    And move out quickly.

LUCIUS: I must go, forgive me,
   Milo is waiting.

BYRRHENA: Do not be a student
   Of her dark wisdom!

LUCIUS: I am not a madman!

Exeunt different ways.

Re-enter LUCIUS.

Pamphale magic! I will make her mine,
Then she will tell me, sighing in my arms,
About the dreams of eels, about the longings
Of moths that make them fly into the fire!
No – she may be as angry as Diana,
Better to creep towards her through her helper,
The bright-haired servant. She shall be my teacher!

Exit.

Enter PHOTIS to the kitchen, stirring the pot.

PHOTIS: My daddy was a fisherman,
   He threw me in the sea,
   With a hook through my abdomen,
   Oh misery, oh misery.

   My mummy was a flowergirl,
   She stuffed me in the ground,
   And cut me at the roots to sell –
   Where could a sadder tale be found?

   My brother was a bankrobber,
   He shoved me in his gun,
   And shot me at an officer –
   Still down the wall my blood does run.

   My sister used to scream and shout,
   We argued in the womb;
   To keep her quiet, I moved out
   Into a slightly smaller room.

Tell me who will be to me
Brother sister father mother?
Empty of my family
I am looking for another.

Enter LUCIUS, behind.

LUCIUS: What is she stirring? There are stars in there,
It is the cauldron of the universe
That her spoon moves! I would do anything
To have a taste of that! I must say something!

PHOTIS looks over her shoulder.

PHOTIS: Good afternoon.

LUCIUS: Good afternoon! Disaster!
I should have spoken first! I will not win her.
Powers of darkness rise! But they ignore me,
Why should they bother with a man who dithers,
Gathering women's legs to decorate
The inside of his head? Oh look at her,
This is the engine of the universe,
See how it turns, the frictionless machine!
Everything following the revolving motion
Of her firm hand, she stands and stirs forever
The planets and my atoms in their polka!
I must do something! Standing here in silence
Will start to look insane. How expertly
You stir the pot! It must be very tasty,
What you are cooking!

PHOTIS: It would burn your tongue.

LUCIUS addresses the audience.

LUCIUS: Do you know why these creatures strike me dumb?
It is the hair, it is the hair, my friends,
See how it twists like thickets made of sunbeams,
Like tops of trees that toss their leaves and shine,

As if receiving messages from heaven!
If they were bald I could speak boldly to them.

He touches her hair, he kisses the back of her neck.

Are you a witch?

PHOTIS: Try to move.

LUCIUS: What will you turn me into?

PHOTIS: When are you free?

LUCIUS: Forever.

PHOTIS: Tonight I take you, bones and all,
Downriver to the waterfall
That drops into the sea of hell
Where angels when they fall in love
Tumble by millions from above,
Like rain that falls into a well.

LUCIUS: Tonight.

PHOTIS: Be ready!

LUCIUS: It is night already!

PHOTIS: It is the evening, it is suppertime.
You must sit down, in patient conversation
With Milo and his wife!

LUCIUS: Oh time, go quickly!

Enter MILO and PAMPHALE to table.

PHOTIS serves.

MILO puts all the food onto his own plate.

MILO: It is all tosh. I loathe astrology
With my whole being. Must I sit and listen
While some fat smiling child-molester tells me
That I and fifty thousand million others

Born on the same day, will have fish for dinner,
And fart at midnight? As for Jupiter
And all these sprites and goblins, hags and demons,
Give me some peace! The world we have to live in
Is difficult enough without religion!
Leave fate alone! Let heaven deal with heaven,
And earth with earth. If I can see a man,
And he speaks sense, I can do business with him.
I work the miracle of making money.

LUCIUS feigns extreme tiredness.

LUCIUS: You are so right, sir! But I am collapsing,
Falling apart, I reckon, at the seams.

MILO: Then sleep! But take no notice of your dreams.

Exeunt all but LUCIUS.

LUCIUS: Now life, begin, and prove yourself amazing,
Each night beyond each day's imagination!

Enter PHOTIS with wine, garlanded in roses. She covers the bed and LUCIUS with roses.

PHOTIS: What are you waiting for, soldier?

LUCIUS: I am awaiting orders.

PHOTIS: Do you know the plan?

LUCIUS I think I can remember.

PHOTIS: Are you armed?

LUCIUS: I am armed.

PHOTIS: What are the odds?

LUCIUS: Even. But I am Julius Caesar.

PHOTIS: Attack then!

LUCIUS: There must be clear provocation.

PHOTIS: What about the element of surprise?

LUCIUS: Lost it before I was born!

PHOTIS: Then I will surprise you. Unconditional surrender.

LUCIUS: (*Turned off by this.*) Oh.

PHOTIS: No? Very well then –

She makes to leave.

LUCIUS: Stand your ground!

PHOTIS: I defy you!

LUCIUS: Well then, since diplomacy has broken down, we must proceed by other means!

PHOTIS: Help help, the barbarians are attacking!

LUCIUS chases her into the bower.

They climb into the rose bower she has created.

Enter LAMATHUS in a bear suit, pursued by dogs and men with spears.

Enter ISIS selling ice-creams and crying 'Ices! Ices!'

LAMATHUS fights with the dogs and men, breaks away, exits.

ISIS exits.

LUCIUS rises.

LUCIUS: Dear friends, last night, without a word of warning,
The full moon crashed into the rising sun,
The mountain maiden and the man of fire
Dragging each other to oblivion
In smoke and steam, her glacier hands descending
His thighs of hot iron; I have gone to heaven,
And all the flowers of the world are crying.

Enter PHOTIS.

My love, sit down!

PHOTIS: Sit down? I've got to sweep the master's dandruff
up off the street, I've got to boil my lady's giblets for the
blithering cats, I've got to catch the chickens and
squeeze some eggs out of them, I've got to chase the
monkeys off the roof and put back the chimney pot, I've
got to make Indian fish dumplings, I've got to cut my
ears off and screw them to the back of my neck and I've
got to build an aqueduct. What are your plans for the
rest of the morning?

LUCIUS: Remembering. When daylight touched my face,
I tried to lift my limbs out of this dreamplace,
But every kiss you gave me, each caress,
Still breathed and brushed their feathers on my flesh –

A hamper arrives.

PHOTIS: What's all this?

LUCIUS: From aunt Byrrhena. 'Come tonight to supper.'
No way.

PHOTIS: No, you should go.

LUCIUS: But I need you, I do not need my aunt.

PHOTIS: Go for supper, slip away after.

LUCIUS: They will not let me, they will talk forever.

PHOTIS: Start screaming and banging your head on the
table.

LUCIUS: They will confine me to an institution!

PHOTIS: But you must go, I won't be your gilded cage. We
can't just lie here fucking all night and all day.

LUCIUS: Can't we?

PHOTIS: Go out and think about it.

Exeunt.

BYRRHENA's house.

Enter BYRRHENA, BELLEPHERON, APPOLONIUS, POETS, who read to each other. A woman in a long dress dances slowly.

BYRRHENA: Now who will save my nephew from the pit
    Towards whose perfumed arms he skips and leaps?
    Into the bearded cave that promises
    Elysium he peers, oblivious
    To the foul she-bear death whose mouth it is!

BELLEPHERON: You say he lodges at the house of Milo?

Enter LUCIUS in a tearing rush.

BYRRHENA: And here he is! My darling, you have come!

LUCIUS: Yes, I am here. Aunt, thank you for the wine,
    Pig, truffles, chickens and this invitation.
    Is this for me?

He drinks down a glass of wine and starts eating fast.

BYRRHENA: You are in such a hurry!

LUCIUS: I have read fourteen books of poetry
    Today already, and I have assembled
    All the best volumes of philosophy
    Back in my room, where they are waiting for me.
    Also I have been told to see the river
    At dawn, and certain palaces and temples,
    And they are old and always falling over,
    Being rebuilt – they change as quick as children!
    I run to sleep, I hack my dreams to pieces,
    And leap awake. Is this the next course?

BYRRHENA: Nephew,
    If you stop eating, I can introduce you

> To my distinguished friends – no need to study
> Dusty old tomes, philosophy resides
> In this man's spirit – Appolonius,
> Lucius.

LUCIUS: Glad to meet you.

BYRRHENA: And the poet
> Bellepheron.

LUCIUS: I read your book this morning.
> Quite good. Keep writing.

APPOLONIUS: What are your impressions
> Of Hypata?

LUCIUS: The place is sick. Dead bodies
> Lie in the ground for half an hour, then squadrons
> Of frantic women elbow past the mourners
> To dig up bits for spells, and everything
> Is sex, sex, sex, God help us, everyone
> Wants to get changed into a beast of some kind
> For mole-sex, frog-sex, dolphin-sex – no wonder
> All your young people want to be assassins
> Or lunatics, or famous murder victims.

BELLEPHERON: You have a healthy attitude to witches.
> And I could tell a tale if you will listen.

APPOLONIUS bursts out laughing.

> Why are you laughing?

APPOLONIUS: It is just the season!

BYRRHENA: The Festival of Risus, god of laughter!
> I hope that you will find some way to praise him,
> Think up some trick to make the city happy!

BELLEPHERON: He is so quick, so flip and so observant,
> He will not fail to tickle Hypata
> With its own tail!

LUCIUS: I swear by Risus, aunt,
   To make you laugh!

APPOLONIUS: Now let the Festival
   Begin!

BELLEPHERON: It is for Lucius alone
   I tell this moral tale, and not for laughter.
   Lucius, I was once as beautiful
   As you, and roamed the world, all eyes, delighted
   Most by myself! I came to Thesally
   For the Olympic games, but at Larissa
   My cash ran out. The only job on offer
   Was this – to stand guard over a dead body
   That night – he was to be entombed next morning.
   I would be well paid by the dead man's widow,
   That any parts a witch might steal for evil,
   I must make good with my own bits. No problem.
   Night fell. I sat beside my cold friend singing
   Uplifting tunes – and suddenly a weasel
   Was standing in the middle of the chamber.
   I stamped and screamed! The creature disappeared!
   I gave myself the world's most special medal
   For bravery, and fell asleep. At dawn,
   The widow burst into the room, examined
   The corpse, pronounced it whole, and sent me smiling
   Out of the house with gold for doing nothing.
   Proud of my work, I watched as the procession
   Carried the corpse across the market place
   Towards its tomb. Then suddenly a tall man
   Straddled its path! As if possessed, he shouted,
   'This man was murdered and I know who did it!'
   The fellow was a priest and he proceeded
   To utter mystic words. The dead man shuddered,
   Sucked in a sudden gust of air, and, struggling
   Onto one elbow, glared at the assembly
   With eyes of fire! Then suddenly he spluttered –
   'It was my wife, she loves another man!'

Of course she called the corpse a lying demon,
Summoned into the body of her husband –
Then he, to prove he was himself, said this:
Last night the man appointed by my wife
To be my body's watchman, guzzled slumber,
And lay like me stretched out. And then a voice
Rose from the wainscot, wispy as a spider,
Calling me by my name, Bellepheron –
Stand on your dead feet, rise, Bellepheron!

LUCIUS: Bellepheron?

BELLEPHERON: Yes! The dead man and I had the same
name! I stood in horror as he described how I, rising
quicker from sleep than he could from death, stepped
towards the voice! How a hand appeared in the darkness
holding a razor that lopped off my nose and ears and
pressed wax copies into the oozing wounds to keep the
crime unknown! And I could not believe what he was
saying –

LUCIUS: I am not prone to disbelief, but frankly –

BELLEPHERON: It is the truth.

*BELLEPHERON removes his nose. Uproarious laughter from
all the assembly.*

LUCIUS: Thanks for the story. Now I must be off.

BELLEPHERON:
What have you learned from my humiliation?
I did not suffer it again for pleasure!
Sweet child of love, pause on the edge of danger,
And think!

LUCIUS: Wise teacher, you have changed my life!
Never shall I forget this evening's teaching!
Women are witches and I must avoid them
Or I will lose the pieces of myself
That I prize most. Now I am safe forever,
Protected by the jockstrap of this lesson!

BYRRHENA: Well done! Well done!

BELLEPHERON: I have not lived in vain!

He tries to embrace LUCIUS, who dodges.

Where are you going?

LUCIUS: To a life of learning!

Exit LUCIUS. He is on the street, drunk.

Bloody old men, there are too many of them,
Surely in wars it should be them that fight!
They are already dead! The night's half gone!
How dare an old man waste a young man's time?

Enter three burly ROBBERS, trying to lift MILO's door off its hinges.

FIRST ROBBER: Come on lads, heave at it!

SECOND ROBBER: It's thick oak this.

THIRD ROBBER: We need a battering ram.

FIRST ROBBER: One last go, then we're in, cut their throats, take everything. Heave my lads, or never get to heaven!

LUCIUS: That's Milo's house! Almighty Venus, thanks,
For making me your blazing Mars tonight!
I am the light, for Photis I will fight!

He battles with the ROBBERS.

I am in love, you cannot cut me down!

ROBBERS: He's a superman! He's a demon!

LUCIUS kills them, bangs on the door, which is opened by PHOTIS.

PHOTIS: Come in, my love!

LUCIUS: Quick, hide me, I have killed
                                                          them!

She pulls him in.

Morning.

Enter OFFICERS, banging on the door.

FIRST OFFICER: Wakey wakey, rise and shine!

SECOND OFFICER: Be a bit grimmer, Hilarius.

FIRST OFFICER: I love my work, I can't help it! Wakey
   wakey!

Enter LUCIUS.

LUCIUS: Put on the handcuffs, lead me to the Judge,
   I did the crime, but he will hear my reasons.

FIRST OFFICER: Wonderful! The one thing Judges love to
   hear about is reasons to kill people. Murderers are so
   reasonable! But the murderer's reasons for killing his
   victims are the Judge's reasons for killing the murderer.
   Most often!

SECOND OFFICER: You're in it now, son. How do you
   feel?

LUCIUS: Justified.

FIRST OFFICER: You will be, you will be well and truly
   justified by the time we're finished with you. As a man
   who's turned to stone is petrified, a man who's fucked by
   justice is justified – crucified, nullified!

LUCIUS: Why are you standing in the street conversing?

FIRST OFFICER: The secrets of our trade are legion. We
   are trained not to act in a predictable manner. We move
   very fast, and then we move very slow, we listen very
   carefully and then we display complete indifference. We

are able to converse, and, conversely, we can turn around and be totally taciturn. With us you do not know where you stand, and so you sit down, you sit down, and you put your head in your hands.

Enter PASSER-BY.

PASSER-BY: Is this the killer?

SECOND OFFICER: This is the man we are questioning.

PASSER-BY: You're done for!

Exit howling with laughter.

Enter other PASSERS-BY.

SECOND PASSER-BY: Why did you do it?

THIRD PASSER-BY: Look at his evil eyes!

SECOND PASSER-BY: Don't get too close!

THIRD PASSER-BY: I want my children to see this!

SECOND PASSER-BY: Do you think he knew what he was doing?

THIRD PASSER-BY: Of course!

SECOND PASSER-BY: When's the execution?

LUCIUS: Take me to court!

FIRST OFFICER: No – not the court, the theatre!

Enter JUDGE, WITNESSES, CROWD.

Three bodies lie under a tarpaulin.

JUDGE: Because this case attracts such interest,
    I have adjudged it in the public good
    To move this trial from the constrictive courtroom
    To the expansive amphitheatre, noting
    However, that this is not entertainment.

Cheering and hysterical laughter as LUCIUS is brought in.

CAPTAIN OF THE WATCH comes forward. Water-clock is placed on the table.

What is this man accused of?

WIDOW: Triple murder!

JUDGE: Call the first witness!

CAPTAIN: Folk, I am the captain
    Of the night watch; I came across this fellow
    As I was in pursuance of my duty
    In the small hours this morning. He was hacking
    The life out of these three Thessalians.
    Citizens hear me! Save our ancient city,
    That good old lady, ravished by a stranger,
    A man from Athens, where they kill their thinkers!

JUDGE: If the accused has anything to say,
    He may now answer to the accusation.

LUCIUS is weeping but manages to get control of himself.

LUCIUS: Am I foreign? Yes I am foreign. I was born
    foreign! It depends on where you are, doesn't it? Well I
    am here, I am here, I am here. I had been drinking – I
    am not used to drinking, not till I came to Hypata have I
    ever been a drinker! Ask my aunt Byrrhena – she thinks
    the world of me – so would you if you knew me! I am in
    love! Also I was bewitched! Have mercy! They are the
    killers, they came at me, three at once. They were going
    to murder my girlfriend. She loves me. One of them
    threw a rock at me. The other one bit me in the leg.
    Look! I ripped his guts out! I was trying to save you, all
    of you!

FIRST CROWD-MEMBER: He's a madman!

SECOND CROWD-MEMBER: He's a child!

THIRD CROWD-MEMBER: Let him go, crybaby!

General laughter. LUCIUS sees MILO and gestures to him.

MILO howls with laughter.

JUDGE: Now we shall hear the widows of the victims.

Enter WIDOWS of the victims.

FIRST WIDOW:
> The clock struck one. He should be home, I reckoned.
> And then the knocking of the officers.
> I speak for us, my sisters cannot speak,
> They are, I think the doctor says, depressed.
> It is for you to give us back to us,
> Help us to close the file, sweet citizens,
> So we can move on. To my little son,
> Who asks me what will happen to the man
> Who killed his father, shall I answer, 'Nothing'?

CROWD: String him up! Cut his balls off! Rip his guts out!
> Bury him alive! Drown him in acid!

JUDGE: He is condemned, and will be shortly slaughtered,
> But I cannot believe that these three mountains
> Could have been shattered by one man from Athens!
> Therefore it is expedient for us
> While he can still speak, to illuminate
> The question of this man's accomplices.
> This is the moment. Fetch the instruments!

Torture implements appear.

Crowd goes wild with excitement.

FIRST WIDOW: Stop! There is still some mercy in this place;
> We must stamp out this flame before it warms us!
> I have seen mothers in the gallery
> Weeping for this young man who is so handsome!
> To see him truly, see what he has done!
> Then choose the method of his execution!

JUDGE: You must remove the cover from your victims.

FIRST WIDOW: So we can all be beasts, as you have been!

LUCIUS: I will not do it.

JUDGE: A hundred thousand people think you should.

LUCIUS: I will not do it.

FIRST WIDOW: Why will he not exhibit his achievements?

LUCIUS: Leave them there! That is their place! Leave them! Please believe me, I was alone! Do not torture me! Leave them under their covers, leave them, why do you want to put them to shame? Do not torture me! Remember them as they were, clean upstanding men, beautiful men, accidentally massacred. This is a public place. Please do not show them to the people! I love them!

He goes down on all fours and starts whining and barking like a dog.

The crowd roars with laughter.

JUDGE: At our mind's limit we are beasts, I notice! Heel, boy! Up, boy! Roll over, boy! Good boy!

He speaks sternly to LUCIUS.

You must obey. You have no other option.

LUCIUS comes to himself.

LUCIUS: Mother! Mother! No, no, no, no, no, no, no, no.

He joins in the laughter at himself, and, crying at the same time, uncovers the corpses. They are blown-up goatskins. The crowd outdoes its former laughter.

LUCIUS stands absolutely still.

JUDGE claps him on the back and kisses him, as do the widows.

CROWD starts to file out, shaking his limp hand.

FIRST CITIZEN: Got you there!

SECOND CITIZEN: That was great!

THIRD CITIZEN: Better than the theatre any day.

FOURTH CITIZEN: That was reality!

FIFTH CITIZEN: Fooled yer!

MILO approaches LUCIUS.

MILO: Last night I saw you slaughtering the goatskins!
 You went to bed still thinking they were robbers,
 You were so slaughtered, so it struck my mind
 To make you this year's sacrifice to Risus!
 Thank you, my friend, my guest! You may consider
 Your bed and board so far entirely paid for!

Exit.

BELLEPHERON approaches.

BELLEPHERON: Young man, did you not listen to my story?
 It was a warning! You are on the brink
 Of some stupendous blunder? Think, oh think!

LUCIUS screams.

LUCIUS: Leave me alone! God help me! Venus, help me!

Exit.

Exit BELLEPHERON.

Enter LUCIUS and PHOTIS. She has a whip behind her back.

Now I will never take you to my bed
And do the things that we have done, again.

Find someone else, I am incapable,
I have been soured by laughter, I am wrecked!

PHOTIS: Oh Lucius, lover, it was me that got you into this!

LUCIUS: What do you mean?

PHOTIS: She's a cat, a slut, a vixen and a thief, she's a shit, a bat, she's a bitch on permanent heat. She's a vicious little frig and I hate her guts and I'd like to drown her in her own piss!

LUCIUS: My love, my love! Who are you talking about?

PHOTIS: At the moment, she's in love with this blond bloke and she saw him getting his hair cut and she jabbed me in the ribs and hissed, 'Get me some of that and I've got him.' But as I reached out to get some, the hairdresser stamped on my hand and I ran off with nothing. But suddenly what should I see but this wineskin-maker shaving goatskins, so stupidly, not wanting to go home empty-handed, I grabbed some of the hairs and ran home, and thrust them into her majesty's hot palm. In the middle of the night on her sacred fire she burned some, but instead of the blond one hammering on her door with his trousers down, it was the three goatskins – and you bumped into them, pissed as a snake, and sweetly killed them, you brave man! So you see I am to blame!

LUCIUS: My God! I see! You mean her magic works?

PHOTIS: Lucius, beat me!

LUCIUS: I shall not fall into the jaws of laughter
Ever again! I shall be armed with horror,
I see how things proceed in Hypata,
All men bow down before the powers of darkness,
Captains and Judges, a whole amphitheatre
Of law abiding citizens and matrons,

41

Helpless with pleasure, roaring at the glory
Of me undone by spells! Well I will join them!

PHOTIS: What do you mean, love? It was just a kind of
accident.

LUCIUS: I want to be a witch! You have to help me!
To be respected – no, to be adored
In Hypata, to turn around the laughter,
Make it flow back to me as gold, a mansion,
Your love forever sure, I need dark powers!

PHOTIS: Don't do it! Look at my mistress, she was lovely
once, her magic has turned her into a permanent serpent –

LUCIUS: Whisper it low, what everybody knows,
You have to cast off kindness, be unsparing
Of others and yourself, you have to enter
The marketplace of darkness and exchange
Heaven for everything you want! Oh woman!

PHOTIS: What kind of thing were you hoping for?

LUCIUS: To be transformed into a flying creature,
So I can have the freedom of the air
To leave my mockers on the ground, appalled,
As I rise out of sight, explore new spheres,
Bring back for your delight unearthly treasures!

PHOTIS: I'll lose you! You'll flutter off and that'll be the
last I'll see of you!

LUCIUS: My love, I will return to you, I swear,
By the eternal tangle of your hair
In which I lie entwined, my nest is here!

PHOTIS: Oh God! She would suck my guts out – she's a
strange and dangerous beast, she's a cow with fangs,
she's a bitch with a tail that stings; she is furry and spiky
and venomous; but fuck her, I love you, I will do this for
you! When she's next up on the roof, that's her place; she

has a platform, facing to the east, that's where she goes when she changes into things.

LUCIUS: My love!

PHOTIS: My love! Now I have set you free, You can do anything you like with me.

They go to bed.

Enter PAMPHALE to her roof.

PAMPHALE: This city is a mountain valley where young men shine like wild flowers; I, the bee, fly from one to the other. So I spread the web of my influence, for I am also the spider. I am the whale in the net, that breaks it, I am the mole that goes under all barriers, I will be all things, I am the sycamore bursting through the floor of the kitchen! Oh pitiful rivals, without the power that is mine, I can scarcely call you women! Oh husband, if you could see me now, what I am about to do! You would jump off the roof, and I would be rid of you. Death has already claimed you, long ago; I could dispose of the body if it would just stop talking! Oh midnight sky, open your bright eye!

She strips and smears herself with ointment. She turns into an owl and flies off.

Enter LUCIUS and PHOTIS in a great hurry, PHOTIS very drunk and giggly, LUCIUS stripping off.

LUCIUS: Help me!

PHOTIS: Which one is it? Which one is it?

LUCIUS: This pot is empty. Find another one!
Break open every box the witch has hidden!
I will suck venom, lick the heads of toads,
Eat things that grow from graves, chew panthers' gallstones!
How many do I take the first time?

PHOTIS: One!

LUCIUS: Oh – one thing – how do I change back again?

PHOTIS: Yes, I don't want you all pecky and feathery. Er –
dill and laurel leaves in well water. Drink it and wash in
it. I'll have some ready and waiting.

LUCIUS: Now I am standing on the highest mountain,
Ready to fly or die! Goodbye, my darling!

PHOTIS: Nothing's happening!

LUCIUS: I feel the change! Now I must leave you, ground,
Soiled blanket that the cold world huddles in!
Where rain divided by the sword of light
Makes colours out of nothing, I will shine!

*He flaps his arms and hoots, and runs off, leaping. His hooting
turns to braying.*

PHOTIS laughs uncontrollably.

PHOTIS: What on earth's happening to your face? Get a
grip on your lips –

LUCIUS: (*Off.*) Can you see my beak?

PHOTIS: You're blowing up – don't burst! Your arms are
turning into legs! Watch your feet!

LUCIUS: Claws, claws!

PHOTIS: This isn't feathers, mate, you're getting covered
in doormat. Nice tail! What's that? Your – oh my God,
this is incredible!

LUCIUS: Do not be sad, my darling, if I shrivel –

PHOTIS: No, no, take a look at yourself! You're enormous!
Oh my darling!

LUCIUS: Why can I not fly? Why am I still standing?

PHOTIS: It was the wrong box! Chaos! Disaster! Madness! But look at the size of that!

LUCIUS: What have you done, my love, what have you done?

PHOTIS: What?

LUCIUS: What have you done –

PHOTIS: Don't try and speak! I've turned you into a donkey.

LUCIUS: Turn me back!

PHOTIS: Eh? What's that in Greek? Don't bray, I'm trying to think! We're dead mice if the owl comes back. God, we're really in it, better do something quick. Why do things always wait till you're pissed to go wrong?

LUCIUS: Turn me back!

PHOTIS: What's the antidote? She did tell me once.

LUCIUS: You mean you don't know!

PHOTIS: Roses! You have to eat roses!

LUCIUS: Get me roses then!

PHOTIS: Hush my love, don't bray, I'll put you in the stable while I look for some roses –

LUCIUS: I'll put my hoof through your face!

PHOTIS: Roses for my sweetheart!

LUCIUS: How can you be laughing?!

Exeunt.

Enter CLYTUS and ARISTOMENUS.

CLYTUS: Turned into a donkey?

ARISTOMENUS: Not a donkey, an ass.

CLYTUS: Ass my arse. Dribbling rivers of nappy-mess. Orchestrated broadsides of unmusical guff! Entire camped armies of bottom-talk! I'd rather be blind and deaf, I'm suffocating, give me a gasp of truth!

Enter ARISTOMENUS

ARISTOMENUS: I have something to tell you, Clytus.

CLYTUS: Oh not you! Give me a break!

ARISTOMENUS: I will. You can have fifteen minutes.

CLYTUS: A likely story!

ARISTOMENUS: Take it or leave it.

CLYTUS: Is that the truth?

ARISTOMENUS: Yes and I'll tell you something else –

CLYTUS: Help!

Exeunt, ARISTOMENUS pursuing CLYTUS.

PART TWO

The cave of the robbers in the mountain.

Enter HYPOTROPHUS, DECIUS, ROBARTES, OLD WOMAN and other ROBBERS, drunkenly singing and stamping.

ROBBERS: When Mars comes marching into town
   Then you and I shall weep no more!
   When all the towers come tumbling down,
   Then all the rich men shall be poor
   And you and I will weep no more!

   When all the men in wigs are burned
   Then you and I shall weep no more!
   When all the toffs to tripe are turned
   Then all the rich men shall be poor
   And you and I will weep no more!

   And who will help to cause this fuss
   So you and I can weep no more?
   It shall be us, it shall be us,
   And all the rich men shall be poor
   And you and I will weep no more!

Enter BALBUS, HOSTUS, SEXTUS and others in a downcast state.

BALBUS: What was all that singing about?

DECIUS: Where's Lamathus?

BALBUS: Carked it.

DECIUS: Lamathus! Oh Captain, Captain!

BALBUS: He will never be forgotten. Julius Caesar? An oily barman. Pompey the Great? Very good at tennis. Lamathus, Lamathus, came from nothing! Give me more of that –

HOSTUS: He was an orphan.

SEXTUS: An urchin.

BALBUS: He was scum! He was a stupid ignorant bastard and he rose to be the Captain of this band!

HOSTUS: He was a soldier.

DECIUS: (*Drinking.*) He stopped us drinking.

BALBUS: He was the stuff of emperors but he was born too late too soon in the wrong place with the wrong face and the wrong friends and the wrong brain.

DECIUS: We are lost! We must disband!

HOSTUS: No – we must stand firm, in memory of Lamathus!

BALBUS: We are not a gang, we are the knights of Lamathus, sworn never to lay down the sword till we have made this empire understand us.

DECIUS: Oh Lamathus, Lamathus!

HYPOTROPHUS: Look at us, we brought back this trunk of loot and you didn't even bring back Lamathus!

BALBUS: We've brought back an ass and a horse and all this!

DECIUS: But woops – you forgot Lamathus!

HYPOTROPHUS: You should have fought to the death!

ROBARTES: We would have done!

BALBUS: If you did what we did, none of you would have come back!

ROBARTES: Yes we would!

DECIUS: That was you! This is us!

ROBARTES: I would have come back!

HYPOTROPHUS: So would I!

DECIUS: I would!

ROBARTES: No – we'd have lost one at least.

HYPOTROPHUS: Who?

DECIUS: Not me.

ROBARTES: Not me.

HYPOTROPHUS: Not me, mates!

ROBARTES: I'm sorry, Hypotrophus.

HYPOTROPHUS: I would have come back!

DECIUS: Not all of us could have made it, mate!

HYPOTROPHUS: I would have come back!

ROBARTES: You've got to go sometime. Face it.

HYPOTROPHUS: Shut up!

They fight.

HYPOTROPHUS is killed.

Enter OLD WOMAN.

OLD WOMAN: Ah my boys! Back safe! No harm can come to those who do good. Look at this beautiful donkey and this wonderful horse! Where did you get them?

SEXTUS: Hypata. House of Milo.

OLD WOMAN: I see! You helped an old man under a mulberry tree, and in return he gave you an acorn and a sycamore seed and said if ever you are in danger, throw these over your shoulder and shout, 'West wind, in my time of need, turn these seeds into galloping steeds!' And when you were chased by the wicked policemen, you did that, and out of the ground sprang this horse and this donkey.

SEXTUS: No.

DECIUS: Tell us what happened to Lamathus!

BALBUS: When I do you'll see why I'm still shaking like a fish in a boat. There is a rich lush called Demochares who collects bears. We found the skin of a dead one and dressed up Lamathus in it and sold him to Demochares. At midnight he climbed out of his cage and started creeping up and down the corridors. But one of the slaves saw him and cried out a pack of hounds, who drove our captain out into the street; then all the boys of the town turned out to pelt him with stones. He never talked, he was a bear to the end. He growled, but he didn't squeal. What a puzzle when they slit that beast open.

DECIUS: We must take courage from the glorious dead!

BALBUS: We have died like beasts, but none of us have died in bed, soaked in his own piss, crying for his mother while the landlord yawns in the corner. (*Finishes his story.*) We made good our losses at Milo's house in Hypata – so Lamathus is happy, he did not die for nothing, he died for nine hundred and eighty-six pounds fifty!

He unloads money into the treasury.

ROBARTES: Oh Mars our father, you have placed our foot
On the soft faces of the hypocrites,
Who deserve worse than even we could give!
In their bronze urns they should be thankful ash
To have been sliced out of their lives by us,
Because we are the justice of the gods!

ROBBERS: Feast! Feast!

They eat.

LUCIUS and his horse are led into view.

The OLD WOMAN feeds them.

LUCIUS speaks to his horse.

LUCIUS: Fortune, you stalk us like a lioness,
    As blind to justice as a falling slate!
    What kind of horror could a man commit
    To be condemned to this, imprisonment
    Inside a dumb beast? What was Photis doing?
    Why was she so slow bringing me my blooms,
    While these corrupt accountants were surrounding
    The house! They loaded all of Milo's treasure
    Onto our backs. Who would have thought the miser
    Had crushing tons of gilded furniture
    Stacked in his attic? And the house was burning
    As we were pricked and bludgeoned up the mountain.
    So much for Photis. Well if she was here
    I'd make her feel the length of my revenge
    On the fouled floor, but it is all too clear
    Fortune hates only me! Or are there others?
    When people vanish, maybe this has happened,
    They have been changed, and can't cry out, I'm human!

Brays.

DECIUS: Shut up, ass!

Kicks LUCIUS.

LUCIUS: Candidus! Candidus! Can you hear me? Can you
    understand me? Or am I completely alone? Ah you
    rascal, you understand every word I'm saying! Keep
    mum, eh? They're watching us. Keep mum. What will
    my feelings be in this condition? What if my needs have
    increased in proportion with my dimensions? What

about you, horse? Do you like women or only horses? What about horsey women? Hey horse, what about our trek up the mountain? Look at my hooves, they've gone splayed, I could make a dash for the pond. A triumphal procession, with our rumps the drums! Were you frightened? No? I was about to collapse but then that other ass that was with us lay down, and when he wouldn't get up they flayed off his skin and rubbed something into his flesh and set light to him. Boom! Must have been gunpowder. We trotted on nicely then didn't we, eh? Like ice in a fat man's pants our weariness melted away. Then I saw a rose, hanging over the track. You know if I eat one of them I'll turn back into a man. You should try it. I reached up my rubbery lips, but then I thought, what would they do to me as a man suddenly sprawling there naked under a load of treasure? Even worse. So I cursed and kept on. But I've got a plan. I'll eat a rose and leap on your back and be gone! When you see me eating a rose, get near me as quick as you can! Watch me at all times! Candidus, Candidus, why don't you speak to mc? I have sung you the epic of my being on lonely roads but now it's your turn! There must be so much you want to tell me! Now is your chance, speak to me!

HORSE: Shut up, cunt.

LUCIUS: So you can speak!

HORSE: Shut up, cunt.

LUCIUS: Say more than that!

HORSE: Off! Get off!

LUCIUS: Believe me, I do not want your barley!

HORSE: Get off! Shut up, cunt! Get off!

HORSE kicks LUCIUS savagely again and again.

LUCIUS: What is the purpose of experience
    If you do not survive its urge to hurt?
    Now I know why the world is full of dirt –
    It is the victim of experience.

He finds a basket of bread.

I am a sky without a world and I
Must fill it up or it will float away.

He eats.

Exeunt some of the ROBBERS.

Dawn breaks.

LUCIUS is still eating.

OLD WOMAN: Good morning, good morning, beautiful
    sun! How freshly you shine on this cave of the blest,
    where no bad thought, and no sad thought can come! A
    slice of bread for breakfast!

*She looks for the basket, finds LUCIUS with his head still in
it, chewing. She screams.*

They'll murder me!

Enter ROBBERS with CHARITE, weeping.

BALBUS: Look at this, lads, we've brought the moon into
    our cavern – gaze on the girl of your dreams – not to be
    touched – if she's yours she's everyone's and there'll be
    nothing left to ransom! Go and write her a poem! Be
    happy, girl, we only took you to remind your father – he
    keeps forgetting to share his good fortune! You are safe
    with us, we're not going to chop off your fingers and
    fuck you to death.

CHARITE weeps all the more.

Old woman! Quiet her down. Where's breakfast?

OLD WOMAN: Oh –

They see the empty bread basket.

BALBUS: Right! Off we go again. You – kill yourself.

Exeunt ROBBERS.

CHARITE: That is what I will do! A rope! Oh donkey!
    I have been stolen from the man I love!

CHARITE throws her arms around LUCIUS' neck.

LUCIUS: But you have found the amazing donkey-man!

CHARITE: We had been married in the afternoon.
    The guests had gone and I was waiting for him.
    The very house was trembling like a bird,
    Shaking the hymen torches! Then these men
    Burst in and I was not to have my husband!

She curls up sobbing and sleeps. He nestles up to her.

LUCIUS: Oh you have lost as much as I have. Girl
    As beautiful as rescue, you have kicked
    My donkey heart out of its dead sleep. Thankyou!
    No, I am not as handsome as I have been.
    Brown eyes like melting sugar, slender fingers,
    Where did you go so quickly? I have taken
    My place among the ugly ones, who frighten
    Their own reflections; if I kissed her now
    I'd stove her head in. Shall we have some tea?
    Woops, bit a chunk out of the cup, demolished
    The table, and your legs – no, I must be
    Frank with myself, this girl is not for me.
    I cannot understand how this can happen,
    Or find its meaning! I have always been
    Wide-eyed for wonders, they have been my teachers,
    But to be kicked and beaten by these madmen
    And my own horse, is that an education?

In his excitement he nudges CHARITE. She wakes up and embraces him.

CHARITE: Husband, oh husband! Jupiter, where am I? Oh yes! Oh no! Tlepolemus, my husband!

She screams.

OLD WOMAN: Stop it! My dear you are spoiling the picnic! Think of your cousins who have gone to such trouble to bring you up the beautiful mountain. Try to enjoy yourself.

CHARITE continues to weep.

OLD WOMAN screams.

Stuff it!

CHARITE: I have!

OLD WOMAN: Alright! Next time I'll set light to your dress.

CHARITE: You seemed so kind.

OLD WOMAN: Sometimes I do strange things.

CHARITE: I dreamed they killed my husband!

OLD WOMAN: Dreams always mean their opposite. Oh dear, dear, dear, do you not believe me? Well if nothing else will comfort you I will tell you a story.

CHARITE: A story?

OLD WOMAN: Listen, all you gnats and bats, you ass, you flies, you rats in the grainbins! Cracks in the walls, widen a little, attend, you ear-shaped stains on the floor; this is a story for you all! Attend, space, attend, time, focus, universe, stop your expanding for I have the story of your soul in my hand! There was once a king who had three daughters – the eldest was striking, the second was a handsome woman, but the third and youngest was more beautiful than Venus – or so people thought! So beautiful she was that the sea stopped when she passed by it and the birds flew straight up out of the universe. Her name was Psyche.

PSYCHE sits on a throne very still like an icon.

She was so beautiful that no man would marry her, but everyone bowed to the ground and adored her as if she was Venus indeed. And the temples of Venus were empty.

Music.

Enter VENUS in fury, with CUPID.

VENUS: This is your duty, my dear child,
    Take up your bow, do not be mild,
    But pierce the strumpet with an arrow
    Through skin and bone into the marrow,
    Infect her with a frantic passion,
    Like it was going out of fashion,
    But let it be for someone vicious,
    Diseased, not in the least delicious,
    Make her desire an oily slicker
    Or an excitable old Vicar,
    Or a mad tramp who shouts all night,
    Or an attractive stalactite.

Exit VENUS.

OLD WOMAN: And Cupid dropped down to the earth. In the meantime Psyche's sisters were married but still no husband could be found for Psyche, and her parents, in despair, consulted the oracle at Delphi.

PYTHIA screams and goes into an ecstatic trance.

PYTHIA: Black! Black! Dress her in black! Let her be dressed in pitch black black! Up, up, take her up, up, put her up on the earth's tooth! A husband for Psyche! A husband for Psyche! He is the rage of the earth, he is the fire of the sky! Sun and moon be slaves to him, God and hell be in his hand! No man, not a man! Dress her in black for her wedding death! A husband for Psyche!

OLD WOMAN: And her parents, in obedience, took Psyche to the top of a high hill and sat her down among the wildflowers and so departed. Strange wedding! And Psyche waited all alone to be devoured by her abominable husband. But then Zephyrus, the west wind, that musician whose flute is the woods and the mountains, picked up Psyche and set her down in a magical valley on a bed of anemones. And there she found a palace made of precious stones, whose doors flew open at her touch; there she was attended by invisible servants who led her to a bed – and there she lay wide-eyed, as the day, beheaded, fell down and darkness ascended its throne. And then she heard something.

Enter CUPID into PSYCHE'S room.

PSYCHE: Something has come into my room.
    The light is out and in the gloom
    I can see nothing. Not one star
    Shines to cast shadows from afar;
    Surely this darkness is divine,
    It sings inside me like red wine,
    Making me brave. I shall not stir,
    Though this could be my murderer.
    What hour is striking with no chimes?
    Who is it that so softly climbs
    Into my bed?

CUPID: I am your husband.

OLD WOMAN: So Psyche loved him many a night, but never never never might she see his face. And this is what she said after the first time, when she woke beside a ruffled place on the sheet.

PSYCHE: Venus, I thank you, now I know
    What makes the pheasant's feathers glow
    And why the cackling magpie shines
    And why the ravens in the pines
    Build their big houses, shout so loud,
    What makes the red deer stand so proud,
    Both hind and stag; and it may be
    That he will not come back to me,
    But he has left me eyes that see!

OLD WOMAN: But he did come back, the invisible, loved
    as deep as the darkness in which he loved; but one night
    he warned her –

CUPID: My love, your sisters are ascending
    The hill you fell from, with heart-rending
    Cries! But you must not call to them,
    Or they will snatch away the gem
    Of our sweet life. They are two twisters,
    Not worth your trust or love!

PSYCHE: My sisters!

OLD WOMAN: She cried all day because, though her
    nights were busy, her days were lonely; and the next
    night he tasted her tears and was persuaded despite
    himself to let her see her sisters.

CUPID: But they will drag you out of grace,
    And make you try to see my face,
    And Psyche, if you look at me,
    Then you will lose me. Do you see?

PSYCHE: That wish shall never come between us,
    Love is the light that comes from Venus,
    And I can see you in my heart,
    So we will never be apart.

    Exeunt CUPID and PSYCHE.

Enter SISTERS to rock.

FIRST SISTER: This is the place! Oh Psyche, Psyche!
    What a catastrophe! Oh crikey!

SECOND SISTER: Sweet sister, I will never see
    Your face again! Poor me! Poor me!

FIRST SISTER: Vile death, return her!

Enter PSYCHE.

PSYCHE: It is me!

FIRST SISTER: Oh! What?

SECOND SISTER: God help us!

PSYCHE: Come and see
    Why you are wrong to weep for me.

ZEPHYRUS carries them down.

OLD WOMAN: So she showed them around the palace of
    her happiness, showed them how her bliss was glass-
    roofed and how artfully her joy was carved and the
    extensions and terraces and conservatories of her
    contentment and its water features. And all the time they
    hissed with joy and gaped their congratulations, but they
    were looking for cracks, they were all eyes for
    woodworm and the tick of the deathwatch beetle would
    have been a heavenly anthem, for though they inhabited
    terrifying masonry mountains, their hearts were little
    hovels of hatred with fake tiling.

FIRST SISTER: Tell us about your lovely husband!

SECOND SISTER: What does he look like?

PSYCHE: Old but kind.
    I love him mostly for his mind.

FIRST SISTER: Is it a big one?

PSYCHE: Shall we have some tea?

While she gets tea the SISTERS speak behind her back.

FIRST SISTER: Can you believe the cutlery?

SECOND SISTER: Sister, I hope I never see
Such an obscene display of money
Again.

FIRST SISTER: It isn't even funny.

SECOND SISTER: I have to tell you something odd –
Our sister's husband is a god.

FIRST SISTER: It is not right!

SECOND SISTER: It shall not be!
Unfairness splits the family!

OLD WOMAN: And they cross-examined Psyche about her
husband's appearance, and when her description was
contradictory –

FIRST SISTER: (*Aside.*) My God – she has not seen his face!
(*To PSYCHE.*) It is a monster! The disgrace!

OLD WOMAN: And Psyche confessed the truth that she
had never actually seen her husband!

SECOND SISTER: Sister – your husband – can you say
Why he will not appear by day?

FIRST SISTER: Is it because he is a snake?
Have you been making a mistake?

Exeunt SISTERS.

PSYCHE approaches sleeping CUPID with lamp and razor.

PSYCHE: What have I been kissing here
In the darkness with no fear?
And the fern that's curled inside,
Is it growing dragon-eyed?

I will light the lamp to see
What has been so free with me.
Now it is your turn to bleed.

She lights the lamp and sees CUPID.

OLD WOMAN: And the flame of the lamp leapt up with
joy to see – Cupid! Her husband was Cupid, who, when
his mother had sent him to curse Psyche, had fallen in
love with her himself and, pricked by his own arrow,
ravished her away to his palace. It was Cupid, stretched
out in sleep, and the razor went blunt from
embarrasment and, longing to touch the god, a drop of
oil jumped out of the lamp!

*PSYCHE desperately tries to put the light out and hide the
razor.*

*The lamp sputters and burns CUPID with oil. He screams
and leaps up. He flies off with PSYCHE holding onto his
legs.*

She drops to the ground, exhausted.

CUPID flies up into the top of a cypress tree.

CUPID: You did not listen! Oh my heart,
You and I must live apart,
Since you needed so much light
In the middle of the night.

Exit.

OLD WOMAN: She wanted to know too much too soon!
And she lost everything!

Enter RIVER. She jumps into his arms.

PSYCHE: I will jump into the river!

RIVER: Sweetheart, it would make me shiver
If I let you sink in me!
Sit beneath this willow tree.

He sets PSYCHE on dry land, sobbing, wandering.

Enter SISTERS.

FIRST SISTER: Sister, what is this misery?

PSYCHE: I lit the lamp but did not see
    A monster – it was Cupid son
    Of Venus, and he cried, 'Undone
    Is all our love, my shoulder blisters,
    I must be married to your sisters!'

SISTERS: To us? You promise? Say no more!

OLD WOMAN: And they ran to the cliff, and, as they leapt,
    cried to the west wind to swoop them down to Cupid,
    but the west wind was just the west wind –

They run and jump off the cliff and are killed.

And Psyche ranged from country to country as if
possessed, praying and crying! She would sweep the
floors of old temples, and so it was that Athene and
Demeter appeared to her one day and told her that since
she had offended Venus, it was Venus that she should beg
for forgiveness! So at last she embraced the altar of the
great Mother, and Venus appeared, like a raging fire, and
commanded her servants Grief and Despair to seize
Psyche and flog her.

PSYCHE is whipped.

VENUS: Daughter in law, I love you dearly,
    Thanks to your passion I am nearly
    A grandmother! I know you yearn
    To see my son. Well you must earn
    The right! I have a job for you,
    Which is not difficult to do;
    You must unmix this heap of grain
    And sand. I will be back again
    In half an hour! (*Exit.*)

PSYCHE: My life is over!

OLD WOMAN: It was not just sand and grain, it was wheat,
    barley, millet, poppy seeds, pease, lentils and beans all
    mixed together. Psyche sat stunned, with the blood
    dripping down her skin. Then suddenly, out of invisible
    holes in the walls came running hundreds of thousands
    of little pismires, emmets, black ants and red ants, the
    little civilized insects, coming with their organised
    minds and their no-nonsense, getting-on-with-it, can-do
    attitude to sort out the mess love made!

Enter ANTS.

And they did it on time and off they went, unpaid, to
    volunteer for the next crisis.

Exeunt ANTS.

Re-enter VENUS.

VENUS: All by yourself? Well done, well done!
    But you have only just begun;
    Before you get to see my son
    I have another chore for you;
    Dear piece of dirt, you must pursue
    The rivers Cocytus and Styx
    To their high mountain source – no tricks
    Will help you with this work – and take
    Enough to splash a face awake!

VENUS gives PSYCHE a cup for the water.

PSYCHE: Now I can either drown or fall –
    Death is not difficult at all.

OLD WOMAN: And she was about to throw herself into
    another river, but a reed spoke to her and urged her not
    to stand against the storm; and Psyche bent, and walked
    right up the mountain to where the rivers begin that
    plunge into the world of the dead under the ground – but

the spring was guarded by long-necked dragons and the waters themselves cried out –

Waters: nightmarish roaring sound.

Her soul was an icicle hanging from the roof of her skull. She could not move. She could not even dream of dreaming. Then suddenly Jupiter's bird, the eagle, happening by, swooped down, took her vessel! Bold fellow, he fixed his sights on a gap between the dragons and dived and scooped up a jarful for the pregnant woman standing by the spring of death's river on the merciless mountain.

EAGLE brings jar to PSYCHE.

PSYCHE: Thank you.

EAGLE: No problem, pretty lady.

Exit EAGLE.

OLD WOMAN: And she placed the jar in the hands of
    Venus.

VENUS: You were not meant to do that. Well,
    Now you must travel down to hell
    And pop into this box for me
    The beauty of Persephone,
    As much as she will give you – say
    Enough to last me for a day,
    For I am going to a play.

OLD WOMAN: And a whole new species of despair
    evolved in her and colonised her thoughts in the
    geological age of one blink.

PSYCHE: Now I shall climb this empty tower
    And end my efforts like a flower
    Flung from her hair into the dust
    By a tall woman in disgust!

OLD WOMAN: Then the tower spoke.

TOWER: From falling there is no return,
 If you jump off, your bones will burn.
 How will your husband kiss the smoke
 That rises from your pyre? Poor bloke,
 To have a wife of ash and cinders,
 Forever slipping through his fingers!

OLD WOMAN: And the tower told her how to reach the
 dead land, and Psyche descended and the Queen of the
 Dead put a smile into the box, and the girl half sleep-
 walked back up into the light. But now she knew she
 would see her beloved, how could she not want just a
 little of the contents of the box for herself to refresh his
 love when he first set eyes on her after such a long time?
 But the beauty of Persephone was the beauty of death.
 Too perfect for the eye of the mind.

PSYCHE opens the box and falls asleep.

But now Cupid in the room where his mother had locked
him, fully recovered from his wound, climbed out of the
window, found his wings and stooped to the place where
his wife lay swooned.

CUPID: Again my love you had to see!
 Surely this curiosity
 Will be the death of you, my dear;
 But I will save you, do not fear.

OLD WOMAN: And she took the box to Venus – and
 Venus was almost pleased with the girl – but still she
 managed a scowl and Cupid cried out!

CUPID: Jupiter, I appeal to you!
 Great King! With love I shall undo
 All human ties, I shall break nations,
 Scramble all rankings and gradations,
 If you deny me Psyche! Wake her,

Or I will make you love a faker
Or a decrepid witch! Great Judge,
Release me from my mother's grudge!

Enter JUPITER.

JUPITER: I fear you, boy. Infinity
Shrinks when you pierce it. When you prick me,
There is no shape I will not take
To get down to the world and make
Love to those girls before they die;
This is my everlasting cry –
When we love mortal people, why
Should it be us that falls, not they
That rise? Well this shall be the day.

VENUS relents.

PSYCHE wakes.

Psyche arise! The world has spoken
In favour of this passion, broken
By Venus only briefly. Now
To Psyche let all heaven bow,
See what this girl has struggled through;
By tears she made the whole world new,
When everything on earth rose up
Against the death of love! The cup
Of victory is hers, our prize –
In peace at last the boy's bow lies!
Heaven attend! It is my judgement,
That for an everlasting moment,
Psyche shall be immortal Cupid's wife,
And love shall be their life!

*GODS and GODDESSES and CUPID and PSYCHE
dance.*

OLD WOMAN: And after a little more happiness, she
brought forth a child, a little daughter, and they called
her Joy.

PSYCHE: When I began to love
    I was a mile behind my life,
    Although I was a happy wife
    I did not know what of;
    I was a cupboard full of light,
    All locked away and out of sight,
    I lost what I had not yet had,
    Then I began to love like mad,
    My life had flown above.
    But by this latest kiss
    At last I know it was like this
    When I began to love.

OLD WOMAN: (*To CHARITE.*) So you see, everything will
    be alright my pretty, why, nothing can stand in the way
    of true love. If your love is true, you will be saved, the
    very dust of the ground will come to your aid, nails and
    screws will cry out in their toolboxes, because when it
    comes to love, we are no different from the gods and
    goddesses, we are everlasting, even this filthy old ass
    could grow wings and fly away with you to your true
    love! Couldn't you, Lucius?

LUCIUS: You said my name! Can you smell my soul
    through this filth? Then you must be a witch, or
    someone with power to put my spirit back into its proper
    body! Look, the time has come, I have learned my
    lesson. In the story I am Psyche, I did everything wrong,
    I tried to see what should not be seen; but I have
    endured my trial, I have lost my beauty and been beaten
    – I am wise now, and I understand everything. Do not
    make me suffer anymore. I cannot stand it in the dung
    much longer!

OLD WOMAN: He brays so nicely, you'd almost think he
    was speaking!

    *CHARITE breaks a vase over the OLD WOMAN'S head
    and jumps on LUCIUS' back.*

CHARITE: Escape! Escape! This is the flight of Psyche!

LUCIUS gallops away with CHARITE on his back.

Beautiful ass! You are a famous racehorse,
Carry me down the mountain to my husband
And I will keep you in a golden stable
And stroke your grizzled muzzle; I will braid
Your tail with red string, I will hang your bridle
With silver bells, you will be beautiful,
I love you ass!

LUCIUS: And I will save you, Lady!

CHARITE: This is a crossroads. Which way down the
mountain?

LUCIUS: Left.

CHARITE: I think right.

LUCIUS: But you are wrong.

CHARITE: Dear donkey,
You have been sweet so far but if you fight me,
We might fall out.

LUCIUS: But that is not the way!
How can you be so stupid?

CHARITE: Bloody donkey!
Do what I want, and I will treat you nicely!
Otherwise I will find a spike and puncture
Your stinking skin!

LUCIUS: If you do that, my beauty,
Then I will shrug you off my back and sweetly
Step on your pretty face.

CHARITE: Come on! God save me!

LUCIUS: Try with your whole mind, struggle to imagine
That there could be a glimmer of a fraction
Of a half chance that you might be mistaken!

CHARITE: Do what I say!

LUCIUS: Atrocious bitch!

CHARITE: Castration!

Enter ROBBERS, ROBARTES, HOSTUS, SEXTUS, BALBUS, DECIUS.

BALBUS: What have we here?

DECIUS: Thief! That's our ass!

They beat LUCIUS back to the cave.

BALBUS: Justice! Justice against this cow and this ass who have tried to rob us of the just rewards of our work!

ROBBERS: Justice! Justice!

BALBUS: The old woman shall hang for this.

They see the OLD WOMAN hanging.

SEXTUS: She's done the job for us.

BALBUS: I cannot condemn this pair by justice for what we would do ourselves. Let no one blame this young woman for stealing herself from us. Whoever does that, accuses all of us. Very well then, I condemn her by injustice, for stealing from thieves. She shall be unjustly punished. Now to the sentence.

HOSTUS: Burn them alive!

BALBUS: That is a legal punishment. That would be justice. My hands are tied.

SEXTUS: What kind of death has not been used by justice?

DECIUS: Work them to death for nothing.

HOSTUS: There's no law against that.

BALBUS: Cut the donkey open and carry it to the top of the mountain. Stuff the girl inside it, and then sew it up again.

SEXTUS: What a great illegal mind!

BALBUS: Let the sentence be carried out immediately.

CHARITE starts to scream.

The knives are sharpened. The ROBBERS are about to slice open LUCIUS.

LUCIUS: Why was I so slow? Why did I not seize
All of creation when I had my hands?
I tried, but Fortune lay in wait for me,
Kicked me down the steps of the Temple of Mockery,
When after years of loneliness love found me,
Fortune shrieked, stamped, spat blood in jealousy!
We must be quick, if we are to enjoy
The glory of this life, we must be cobras,
Ospreys – above all, we must not be donkeys!

Enter ALEXANDROS.

ALEXANDROS: Comrades!

DECIUS: Alexandros!

ALEXANDROS: Where's Lamathus?

BALBUS: Fixing the roof.

ALEXANDROS: Place feels a bit big without him! Mates, I met a man on the road, six-footer, foaming at the mouth, sick to death of working. I said why not join my army?

BALBUS: Show him in!

ALEXANDROS gestures to TLEPOLEMUS to come in.

ALEXANDROS: This is the man!

TLEPOLEMUS: God bless this place! Ah, God, I would rather have a cave for my billet than lay my head between the legs of the empress!

BALBUS: He speaks like Lamathus.

SEXTUS: Where have you come from?

TLEPOLEMUS: Out of an old song. Are you thinking maybe I am a god? I am not bothered with gods. Except for Mars, lads!

DECIUS: You are not from these parts.

TLEPOLEMUS: My father was Theron. Theron! You have heard of Theron! Now he is a stain on the ground.

HOSTUS: What happened?

TLEPOLEMUS: The emperor sent a legion.

SEXTUS: Why so many?

TLEPOLEMUS: Because of something we had taken.

ROBARTES: What had you taken?

TLEPOLEMUS: Macedonia.

BALBUS: Theron Caesar!

TLEPOLEMUS: Till his empire dwindled to the top of a mountain, slopes thickly forested with soldiers. But I, like Achilles, put on a dress and rode off on a donkey.

ROBBERS: Wahey!

TLEPOLEMUS produces the dress.

TLEPOLEMUS: The start of my career as a dancer. In which I have lifted millions.

The dress is full of coins. He showers them onto the ground.

BALBUS: Captain! Captain!

TLEPOLEMUS: Well since you ask so nicely.

ROBBERS cheer.

We will suck up the cities of the earth like prunes, we will get that withered little emperor who killed my father, and we will make that bastard dance in taffeta!

He unloads a sack full of food and jars of wine.

Music.

He dances in his dress up to CHARITE.

And who are you? Will you be free with me?

CHARITE: I have not had my last dance yet, I see.

They dance.

LUCIUS: I never could have dreamed what I have seen
Since I was turned into an ass! This maiden
Has just been told that she is to be auctioned,
And she is skipping like a schoolgirl, laughing
And dancing with this unconvincing brigand!
I am more beast than I have ever been,
Having seen this! I am betrayed, demeaned,
Transformed! How could you do this to me, woman?

Suddenly all the ROBBERS fall down asleep.

TLEPOLEMUS: Goodnight!

CHARITE: Tlepolemus!

TLEPOLEMUS: Wife!

They embrace

My love.

CHARITE: My love. You must give thanks to this ass – he tried to help me to escape!

TLEPOLEMUS: Homewards! This ass will be a famous ass!
 When you have ridden through the city gates,
 We will proclaim him to the citizens,
 The great escape ass, who in his attempt
 Almost pre-empted bold Tlepolemus!

They start to ride towards the city, CHARITE on LUCIUS.

CHARITE: And he must be rewarded!

TLEPOLEMUS: He will have
 A herd of wives – and he will ride tonight!

CHARITE: Our wedding night was not our wedding night.

TLEPOLEMUS: Our second wedding shall complete the first;
 Look at the people streaming from the city
 In jubilation to complete our wedding!

Enter people celebrating.

LUCIUS: To save her life he turned into a thief.
 Getting my way I turned into a donkey.
 I deserved this disgrace. But it is over,
 I will eat roses when we reach the city!

TLEPOLEMUS: (*To GROOM.*)
 Now introduce this donkey to his wives;
 And he must do no work, he is retired.
 He is the bravest donkey in the world,
 And he shall have a statue in our town!

CHARITE: Beautiful donkey, I will visit you,
 And we will talk about our wedding nights
 Tomorrow. Glory! Victory! Victory!

Exeunt all but LUCIUS and GROOM.

GROOM leads LUCIUS to the mares.

GROOM: Well I do reckon this be donkey heaven.

GROOM stands grinning and guffawing.

Goo on! Har har har! Goo on!

FIRST MARE: Is it true that you galloped away with Charite?

SECOND MARE: And they've given you us to reward you?

THIRD MARE: You were so brave!

LUCIUS: Any ass would have done it. There was a horse there – big fellow, but he didn't move. I could see it was up to me, ass though I may be, it just had to be done, that's all there is to it.

FIRST MARE: You're terribly big for a donkey!

LUCIUS: I can eat roses any time I want to –
Might as well use the thing I have been given!
Shall we get started? Oh my God, the husbands –

Enter STALLIONS.

GROOM: Ooh eck.

FIRST STALLION: Yes, can we help you?

SECOND STALLION: Have you lost
                                        your way?

LUCIUS: I was just going.

FIRST STALLION: In the wrong direction.

They beat up LUCIUS.

GROOM chases away STALLIONS, leads off battered and braying LUCIUS.

Exeunt.

Enter CLYTUS and ARISTOMENUS.

CLYTUS: Escape! Escape!

ARISTOMENUS: But come back!

CLYTUS: Cup of tea?

Exeunt.

PART THREE

An amphitheatre in Corinth.

Enter the RINGMASTER.

RINGMASTER: Ladies and gentlemen! The moment
you've all been waiting for. It doesn't get any better than
this! What you're about to see has never been seen
before!

Enter LIONS. He pretends it's an accident.

Whoa! Who let them out? Hey! Back, Pompey, down,
Julius!

He whips them off stage.

You'll be seeing them again, don't worry. You will see
everything! Citizens, take a last look at your friends, you
will not be the same when you leave this place today!
And now to introduce you to the main event, here is
none other than the Lord High Chief Justice, patron of
these games, Thiasus!

THIASUS comes forward.

*A condemned woman is brought on, hooded, and tied to a
frame.*

THIASUS: Civilisations do not just decline,
    They blossom into new forms of confusion.
    Citizens, friends! You know that in these times
    Massacre horror and despair are common!
    Judges are going bonkers all the time,
    Unhinged by what they hear! Take this example:
    This wife grew jealous of her husband's cowmaid,
    And made a plot to kill the girl. She had her
    Stripped, and thrust in a red hot iron that killed her;
    Killed her own husband with a dose of poison,

Killed the physician who had sold it to her,
Then her own daughter, since the law declared her
Her father's heiress. How shall this be answered?

Howls of all kinds from the crowd.

*Enter LUCIUS all dressed up in finery and carried on a
litter, eating grapes.*

RINGMASTER: What's this? A donkey eating grapes? Am
I dreaming, ladies and gentlemen? This is ridiculous.
What kind of a fool do you people think I am? This is a
gladiatorial arena – we want blood here!

One of the SLAVES whispers to him.

Oh! He's a dangerous animal, apparently, ladies and
gentlemen – more vicious than a tiger in uniform, as
savage as a senator. He is, in fact, our *belle lettre* – no,
our *pièce de resistance*; and what he will perform here
today for you will leave you sweating forever. But first
he's going to tell some fortunes, Ladies and Gentlemen.
Fortune has made an ass of him, but what about the rest
of us? What lies in store for the woman here?

Picks a card from the pack that LUCIUS holds out.

Oh! Oh no!

SLAVES start to lead LUCIUS towards condemned woman.

SLAVES: Bring him on gently now, come on, come on!

LUCIUS seems bewildered and reluctant.

LUCIUS: I do not know what I am doing here,
But I am sure I have been here before,
Suffering laughter in the amphitheatre,
Mocked because I am not a murderer!
How blissful to be innocent of murder –
We do not know how fortunate we are!
But surely I was not an ass before!

What was I then? An antelope? A zebra?
A beetle? No! I was a kind of person,
A smutty student innocent of murder!
But that does not explain why I am here.
Will no one tell me, out of charity?
Will no one have the charity to tell me?

Amphitheatre freezes.

Enter GROOM with LUCIUS to TIMINOS.

GROOM: This be the ass of our mistress Charite. Here you are, Timinos! I got a job for you lad! No use you sitting there dribbling all day. I know you're not fit for any skilled labour, but seeing this ass is to do no work but only to be pampered, I've picked you to look after him and treat him as your own. Dote on him, Timinos, and feed him on hay, tis the wish of our mistress.

Exit GROOM.

TIMINOS: Charite has given you to me to look after, donkey! Donkey! Donkey! You're my donkey! Up, up, up, up, up! I want to try you out!

LUCIUS: What is this imitation Cupid doing?

TIMINOS picks up a stick and starts beating LUCIUS.

TIMINOS: Whack! Whack! Whack! Hey – this donkey doesn't work! Whack! Whack! Whack! Whack!

He starts moving.

Blip! Blip! Blip! Missed! Blip! Blip! Blip!

LUCIUS: Vary your aim!

He collapses.

TIMINOS: Get up! Get up you punk, you freak! I hate you, I hate you! Aaaaaggghh! Aaaagggghhh! Get up I said!

He starts to cry and scream.

I knew this would happen! My donkey's stopped! Oh!
Oh! You stinking old hands-down-your-trousers!

LUCIUS: I have read the entire works of Aristotle.

LUCIUS gets up out of the stream.

TIMINOS: Here we are, here we are! And I'm going to
load these logs onto your back and you're going to carry
them back down the mountain!

*He starts to load enormous amounts of wood onto LUCIUS'
back.*

LUCIUS: Charite, help! Have you forgotten me?

TIMINOS: (*Piling on wood.*) Aurelia's mother's got tits that
light up in the dark. Apparently. She sits in the window
at night and it's like two burning eyes. Moths come and
flutter all over her. Apparently. She loves it. Bloody
norah, how much can you stand? This is amazing! What
a donkey!

LUCIUS: Now I am dying in a donkey's skin!
And who will know there was a man within?

TIMINOS: Get your little no-arse on the move, boy, before
I tartan your buttocks! I said move, you little misery!
Move! Aaaaaagggghh! Go! Go! Move! Move!
Aaaaaagggghhhhh!

LUCIUS: Why am I taking this so patiently?

He kicks the boy flying.

Oh please be dead! He isn't even stunned!

TIMINOS: I am going to kill you now, mummy. Kill him!
Kill him! Kill the donkey! Aaaaaaaagggghhhhh!

He is about to hack LUCIUS to bits.

Enter SESTOS and ABYDOS, in a panic, stopping him.

SESTOS: Woah there, steady boy! No, boy! Woah there boy!
Down boy!

ABYDOS: Hey there, woah there boy! Steady there boy!
Woah boy!

SESTOS: This be the donkey our mistress did give you to
keep!

TIMINOS: He mounted Flavia's mother in the street! Oh!
Oh! Oh! He's always doing it!

ABYDOS: Do not force yourself to relive the experience.

SESTOS: Well we cannot have that! Tis indecent.

ABYDOS: Cut off his plums.

LUCIUS: Venus! Do not permit this! Build a wall
Of steel around my back legs, save me Venus!

TIMINOS: Can I do it?

ABYDOS: You can watch.

TIMINOS: Do it now!

ABYDOS: I will fetch my instruments.

Exeunt SHEPHERDS.

LUCIUS: Farewell to you forever, pretty maids,
I shall not meet you in my dreams again,
Loiter at my heart's corners to admire
You passing by like walking autumn trees!
And I will feel no wish to be a man.
It was desire that pushed me down, but how
Without it can I get back up again?

*TIMINOS drives LUCIUS up the mountain and begins to
chop wood.*

TIMINOS: This is the way we chop them off,
    Chop them off,
    Chop them off,
    This is the way we chop them off
    On a cold and frosty morning!

LUCIUS: Where are you when I need you, death?

Enter BEAR.

LUCIUS: Who are you?

BEAR: I am the bear, death.

LUCIUS: Who have you come for, me or the boy?

BEAR: Him.

LUCIUS: Why?

BEAR: I do not have to explain that to you.

LUCIUS suddenly goes wild and runs off.

Exit BEAR with TIMINOS.

Re-enter LUCIUS.

Re-enter SHEPHERDS with bits of TIMINOS.

ABYDOS: There is the murderer!

SESTOS: Seize him!

They seize him.

Enter MOTHER of TIMINOS.

MOTHER: Is this the ass that did it? Devil behind the eyes
of this animal, you shall not mock my misery!

She beats LUCIUS with an iron bar.

He speaks as if remembering it as it happens.

LUCIUS: She took the bar that barred the stable door
    And beat my bones till she could beat no more,
    And it fell heavy on the stable floor
    From her slack hands. She stamped and spat and swore,
    And thrust in fire beneath my tail. Too sore
    That is to be remembered. And I cried
    Like a big baby, under my thick hide.

MOTHER: Too weak I am from bearing and burying! You
    will be slaughtered in the morning.

Exit MOTHER.

LUCIUS: Why do they beat me? What is it about me?
    In my opinion this was not a woman
    But a vast system of exploding suns
    Raging and burning in a wrinkled prison!
    This much I learned before my execution.
    But if my mistress comes she can still save me!

Enter RAPSIOS and other SLAVES.

RAPSIOS: She is mad! Stop her! She is mad!

Enter CHARITE covered in blood, with a sword in her hand.

CHARITE: Tlepolemus! I have avenged you, husband!
    This is his tomb, and here he lies cut down,
    So you believe, by a wild boar while hunting
    with Thrasillus our friend!

Enter THRASILLUS with dead body of TLEPOLEMUS.

                    It was this man
    Who brought me the dead body of my husband.
    I entered into mourning and erected
    A statue of Tlepolemus to cry to.
    And Thrasillus would visit to console me.

THRASILLUS: We three were closer than the trinity
    Of Graces. I am lost, a third of me
    Is in the earth. The rest will follow shortly,

Charite, dearest, if I do not say –
It is his wish that you should be my bride.

Exit.

CHARITE: That very night, the statue spoke to me!

STATUE: Marry again, but not my enemy!
   Thrasillus killed me, it was not the boar!
   Give him no inch, he is my murderer!

Turns back into statue.

CHARITE: So I invited Thrasillus to dine
   Last night with me but drugged his wine, that laid him
   Out warm! And from my hair I drew the pin
   And burst the lustful bubbles of his eyes.
   I see my husband on the other side –
   He smiles to me and reaches out his hand.
   Rejoice! It is my wedding day again!

She kills herself.

RAPSIOS and others carry her into the tomb.

ABYDOS: Hard to believe that one strolling so blithely on
   the green slopes of gladness could slip so suddenly over
   the cliff edge of catastrophe.

LUCIUS: Seas of disaster pour into my mind,
   And my big ears like spider's webs are buzzing
   With dying things! I was an honest man,
   Now I am nothing but the dribbling wind,
   That cannot speak except by shaking loose things;
   Venus has got her vengeance on my mind!
   What was it I was meant to do to turn
   Back into what? Eat something – was it hay,
   Thistles – some flower – ragged robin maybe –

SESTOS: Let us sell this ass, Abydos, and with the money
   make our way to another place.

LUCIUS is taken by the SHEPHERDS to market.

AUCTIONEER: What the buggery have you been doing with this one? Well, well, what can I get for this sad ass with a hide like a map of Africa that's been used as toilet paper? If money frightens you, put your minds at rest, don't worry. Do you find it hard to cry, sir? Place this creature in the corner of your garden, and freely weep whenever you set eyes on it. I am stretching the pants of my imagination.

Enter the rich BAKER, Rubicon.

Ah, Rubicon! Just what you're looking for! Yours for next to nothing, then give him one feed and let him turn the mill till he drops. What have you lost?

BAKER: (*To SLAVE with purse.*) Give this man next to nothing.

LUCIUS is sold to the BAKER and tied to the mill, amongst other beaten asses and slaves. He brays.

LUCIUS: What was that noise? That was what I was thinking. Nothing more witty than –

He brays.

Now I am sure I never was a man!
All things believe they were once something better;
Speak to the cows across the fence, they'll tell you
They were once housemaids to the emperor!
What did I do? Smear ointment on my skin
To turn into an owl? A likely story!
Only a donkey could have dreamt up that one!
What can I offer to this whirling courtroom
Other than my own fantasies, the dreams
Of a damned ass whose mind has turned too often!

Enter Baker's WIFE and FRIEND.

FRIEND: Hey, Phyllida, where's your husband?

WIFE: Running the universe!

FRIEND: Where's your young man?

WIFE: Oh he wouldn't come here, he's frightened of my
husband's thunderbolts.

Enter BAKER, snooping. FRIEND spots him.

FRIEND: Your husband? I tell you, my Phylly, with that
man you're the luckiest little lady in the Roman empire.

BAKER: Ah, Sapientia! And how is your husband?

FRIEND: Still dead, Rubicon.

BAKER: I am sorry – the business of the mill – difficult
times –

Exit in embarrassment.

WIFE: They would be difficult times if it was left up to
him. All he thinks about is what I'm doing.

FRIEND: That is because of his misfunction.

WIFE: The imagination's still functioning big time.

FRIEND: It's a terrible shame – look at you, you've got
great skin and your lips are delicious and your hair's full
of body and you've got lovely bosoms; you're a woman
crying out for attention.

LUCIUS: Surely a loaf does not require such torture?
Master, do you not see that we are dying?
Look at the ugly, suffering machine
That makes the bread that makes the baker's living!

Enter LOVER.

LOVER: I have come!

WIFE: What a big brave man!

85

LOVER: Hello Sapientia!

FRIEND: I feel the onset of irrelevance.

Exit.

WIFE: So what brings you then?

LOVER: The gorilla has gone to visit his colleague in the neighbouring cage. I saw him on the road so I nipped in.

WIFE: I still don't understand what you want. Bread, is it, or just flour?

LOVER: I want bread and butter, cut thick, and lots of jam!

They embrace.

FRIEND: (*Off, shouting.*) Hello, Rubicon! Back so soon?

BAKER: (*Off.*) Goodbye, Sapientia, best regards to your husband!

WIFE: Under the trough!

She turns over a trough and the LOVER hides under it with his fingers sticking out.

Enter BAKER.

BAKER: My faithful darling!

WIFE: Eh?

BAKER: Sitting here waiting alone!

WIFE: Why?

BAKER: My poor friend Honorius has just caught his wife having an affair. It happened while I was there! She was entertaining herself with a young man when suddenly Honorius returned.

Enter WIFE OF HONORIUS with her YOUNG MAN.

WIFE OF HONORIUS: Oh my dear sweet young man, I hope my husband does not suddenly return!

YOUNG MAN: Ha ha ha ha ha!

They embrace.

Loud door-sound.

HONORIUS: (*Off.*) Hello, darling! I'm back unexpectedly!

WIFE OF HONORIUS: Venus save us! Under the sulphurator!

YOUNG MAN climbs under a wooden frame draped with cloth, through which fumes are rising.

Enter HONORIUS.

HONORIUS: Bleaching sheets with sulphur fumes, darling?

WIFE OF HONORIUS: It makes them so white, darling.

HONORIUS: And they need it, after some of the things we get up to on them!

YOUNG MAN sneezes.

Bless you darling.

WIFE OF HONORIUS: Thank you, darling.

HONORIUS: Dear, do forgive me for rushing home. I have just heard the most awful story about Nullius – his wife Inertia was having an affair with a young man and she was enjoying herself with him one day when suddenly Nullius returned and she made her lover jump into this big jar. And Nullius said, Congratulate me, darling, I have just sold this jar to so and so, and he's on his way now to collect it; and Inertia comes back, quick as a snake, What do you mean you've sold it, I've just sold it to this gentleman who's inside inspecting it – and the lover cries out, There's a few stains here at the bottom!

So Nullius helps him out and jumps in and starts scrubbing away while the lover takes Inertia up against the side of the jar, and she's moaning out – a little lower – rub hard – more, more – ah, yes! And the lover finishes his job and Nullius finishes his job and Nullius carries the jar round to the lover's house, at no extra cost!

YOUNG MAN sneezes again.

HONORIUS: Bless you again, darling.

WIFE OF HONORIUS: Thank you again, darling.

YOUNG MAN goes into paroxysms of coughing and sneezing.

WIFE tries to pretend it's her.

HONORIUS rushes to save her, realises it's not her, exposes the YOUNG MAN.

BAKER: At that moment I arrived.

HONORIUS: Explain yourself!

YOUNG MAN gasps and pukes.

Drusilla, is this what it looks like?

WIFE OF HONORIUS: Yes it is you old goat.

Exeunt WIFE OF HONORIUS, HONORIUS, YOUNG MAN.

BAKER: At that moment I left, and rushed here in a state. Drusilla is famous for her faithfulness; if she could be an adulteress, why then – ! Oh forgive me, my heart – I will never be suspicious again, we will make a new start.

A SLAVE unhitches LUCIUS and starts to lead him off. He treads on the YOUNG MAN's hand.

YOUNG MAN screams and jumps out.

BAKER: Phyllida, is this what it looks like?

WIFE: Yes it is you old stoat!

BAKER: Oh no! No! No! Oh no!

BAKER breaks down.

Exeunt all but LUCIUS.

LUCIUS: They are all beasts! My friends, do not be shamed
    For being donkeys driven in a round,
    Our masters and our mistresses are chained
    To their own lust, the flour their labours grind
    Is hatred and betrayal, soon to be
    Baked into bricklike loaves of misery,
    Stale from the oven. Then they will be changed
    To beasts of burden just as we have been,
    My love was never better, it was mere
    Chafing of members, like a pig that grinds
    Its arse against a gatepost. I have loved,
    Like a canary singing to its mirror,
    Only myself. But I was only human.

Enter TWO STORIES.

FIRST STORY: Lucius, let me tell you a story!

SECOND STORY: Lucius, let me tell you a story!

FIRST STORY: There was a slave, the steward of a
    household –

SECOND STORY: There was a man who had a son –

FIRST STORY: And he loved a hooker in the town –

SECOND STORY: His son's mother died and he married
    again –

FIRST STORY: And his wife, in fury, piled up all the
    accounts and set light to them –

SECOND STORY: His second wife fell in love with her stepson –

FIRST STORY: Then she took their daughter by the hand –

SECOND STORY: He would not love her back, so she decided to poison him –

FIRST STORY: And went to the edge of an abandoned mineshaft –

SECOND STORY: But by mistake her own son drank the poison!

FIRST STORY: And tied a rope around them both –

SECOND STORY: Then she accused her husband's son of murdering her own son!

FIRST STORY: And jumped.

SECOND STORY: Just when the son was about to be condemned –

FIRST STORY: The master, enraged by the loss of his accounts –

SECOND STORY: An old man stood up in court, and cried out, I sold the poison!

FIRST STORY: Took the servant who loved the prostitute –

SECOND STORY: I sold it to this lady, and if you want proof, listen –

FIRST STORY: And tied him, naked, to a stump, and smeared honey all over him –

SECOND STORY: It was only a sleeping draught! Go to the tomb of this woman's son –

FIRST STORY: The ants in the stump swarmed out and began to eat him –

SECOND STORY: And wake him up!

FIRST STORY: They crawled into his mouth and bit chunks out of his tongue –

SECOND STORY: They did – he woke – and his stepmother was condemned –

FIRST STORY: And slowly bit off all his flesh down to the bones.

SECOND STORY: To be burned. Thanks be to Venus, amen!

FIRST STORY: To Venus be thanks, amen!

Exeunt STORIES.

A scream.

The BAKER is revealed, hanged.

LUCIUS is led away to be sold.

RINGMASTER: Which only goes to show, ladies and gentlemen – it's not what you are it's what you do, it's not where you come from it's where you've been, and what about this donkey, I hear you asking, where did we find this genius, this spirit of the age? Not in a riding academy, not in a school for young ladies –

LUCIUS is seated at a table covered with good things.

Enter THIASUS, MELLITUS, CLYTUS and ARISTOMENUS and other guests.

MELLITUS puts a cigar into LUCIUS' mouth.

He smokes. Everyone applauds. LUCIUS is given a glass of brandy, which he holds with great difficulty, but succeeds in drinking, to rapturous applause.

THIASUS: Our cooks got him for nothing – thought him an ordinary beast but then they caught him one day

browsing on an apricot Danish. Now bring him
something so refined the very idea of a donkey would
make it put on glasses and recite the works of
Bellepheron –

COOK presents a dish to THIASUS.

COOK: Bombay duck.

THIASUS: Oh.

COOK: Bombay duck mouse.

THIASUS: Oh!

COOK: Bombay duck mousse *à l'orange*!

THIASUS: Give it to him!

It is presented to LUCIUS, who gobbles it up.

COOK weeps.

LUCIUS: Friends, this is nothing. Once I ate a man.
He grumbled in my stomach for a while,
And then I shat him out of my back end.

THIASUS: Come drink with me, my friend! From now on
I shall not populate the mad little hours of the morning
with myself alone, I shall look into his eyes and see, at
last, someone as drunk as I am! The possibilities! We
will travel the world, parade through every town, I will
make a fortune!

They set out.

LUCIUS: So in the trappings of an ass of honour
I prance from place to place beneath my master,
And my performance is adored by thousands.
I can do anything you want!

MASSIMA: I want him.

THIASUS: For what kind of work? Oh, my dear lady –

She gives him money.

No man should stand between a woman and her dreams. Be gentle with him.

Exeunt all but MASSIMA and LUCIUS.

MASSIMA: Have no fear. I know what you are.

LUCIUS: I am a donkey.

MASSIMA: You are my love.

LUCIUS: I am a donkey.

MASSIMA: All my life I have been searching for you! Now I will never let you go! Oh my darling!

They go behind a veil.

Enter CLYTUS.

CLYTUS: Stop! This is going too far! Who dreamt up this filth? This is never in the original book!

ARISTOMENUS: Yes it is – look!

He produces a copy of 'The Golden Ass'.

CLYTUS: Is this Apuleius?

ARISTOMENUS: In Latin, yes.

CLYTUS: Can I read this out?

ARISTOMENUS: Be my guest!

CLYTUS: Nunc mulier – oh – now the lady – removed her clothing – and anointed herself with – balsam – which she also applied to me – paying special attention to my – muzzle – (it's hard to get the sense across but I'm trying). Then she – kissed me. And she told me passionately, 'I love you, you are my only one, I cannot live without you.' (And so on.) Then she grabbed hold of my – bridle – and made me lie down. All this came naturally to me, especially since I was flush with red wine – and – egged on by the smell of the balsam – Shall I continue? What worried me though was, the – er – difficulties. How could I – embrace her delicate and tender body – and kiss her soft lips with my huge rubbery ones – rubberaria – and how, quite frankly, was she going to accommodate my preposterous piece – piecus preposterosus – Look I can't go on with this! But I needn't have worried – because – ah! Tumtetum – dadadee – I see – ooh! Mhmn. Tiddleypom. And then – ah, yes. And – ah! So that was alright then!

ARISTOMENUS: You see! And he was a person anyway, really!

CLYTUS: Absolutely!

Veil is withdrawn to reveal MASSIMA and LUCIUS smoking cigars.

MASSIMA:
Why have you stopped the play? Why are you staring
With your mouths open? Have you never seen
Two lovers resting on the mountain top
Of one another? Is our love too much
For you to understand? I have been given
Peace, which I could not find in chariots
Of gold or kings or diplomats or soldiers.
You who are both immense and tender, frightened
And brave, have changed me and I thank you truly.

THIASUS: Yes! He could do this in the amphitheatre!
That would be justice!

Amphitheatre unfreezes.

LUCIUS is being led towards the condemned woman.

RINGMASTER is still looking at the tarot card.

RINGMASTER: Horrible! But I put the blame on Fortune!
    And when the ass has made her his forever,
    The lions shall devour his leftovers!

LUCIUS: I shall not do this! I am not a human!

SLAVES: Bring him on gently now, get him on her – (*Etc.*)

LUCIUS: Citizens of the empire, fellow creatures!
    You are all sailing into devastation,
    Clutching at whores! Friends, I was once a human,
    And it may be that you can hear my warning
    Through this mad braying! Stop what you are doing,
    It is not justice! I can see you changing!
    You are all turning into worse than vermin!
    She who cursed me will not spare you, my friends!
    Repent!

SLAVE: Shut him up! Get a muzzle on him!

Enter LIONS.

RINGMASTER does not see them.

RINGMASTER: Why so shy all of a sudden! Get on her!
    Get on her!

LIONS attack RINGMASTER.

No! Who let them loose again? Felix! Get off my arm!
Down boy – Pompey! Aaaagh! Venus! Not my – oh no –
ladies and gentlemen!

He is eaten.

LUCIUS: I see an open gate. I will go through it.

Exit LUCIUS running.

Re-enter to the seaside. Enter the sea.

Oh hide me ocean from these human lions,
Vultures with hands,

Rats with ambitions!
Men worse than beasts! And I was one of them!

He goes down to the sea.

Sea, you were never an efficient mirror,
But I can see too clearly what I am.
Poor donkey! How I hate you, humble one,
I know that if I was a man again,
I would treat you like they do – beating you,
Beat some poor fellow like myself transformed!
There is no road, no reason to return
Into the clubs and companies of men!
But nor can I remain in this condition!

The moon appears.

He sees its reflection.

What is this question mark without a question?
Oh it is you, moon, rising, full again!
You have seen even more than I have seen,
But still you rise! I see your face has taken
A beating. You and I are just the same,
Our journeys are absurd and neverending,
We look, but things do not like to be seen,
They turn in shame and try to beat us blind!
But you have gained from all your suffering,
You hang so steady, like a decoration
On the night's breast. O blessed queen of heaven,
Forgive me that I do not know your name!

As he speaks he washes himself in the sea seven times.

You have the power to transform all things,
Preserver of the earth, this dirty coin
Your rising rubs clean! So bright is your looking,
You must be Venus who in the beginning
Coupled all things to make life everlasting!
Or are you Ceres who in celebration

Covered the world with corn to save all nations?
Are you severe Proserpina whose howling
Chases the bad dead back into their chasms?
The waves obey you like a flock of lambs,
Running behind you, leaping in your beams,
Changing the edges of the sleeping land.
Now in the salt waves that your face illumines
I have immersed my body seven times!

He falls asleep.

Enter PHOTIS.

PHOTIS: Lucius! Lucius! Is it you, Lucius? It is me, Photis!

LUCIUS: Photis, my love! Photis!

PHOTIS: Nod your head if it's you! Was that a nod? No.
Oh Lucius! Perhaps you have forgotten yourself! Love, I
have been looking for you ever since that night! They
snatched you out of my clutches! I was just getting
started on you, Lucius! I loved you. Do you know
anything that's happened? The thieves knocked Milo on
the head. Pamphale never came back. I was sold to a rich
old git who had the courtesy to snuff it quite quickly,
and he left me my freedom and his geld! Amazingly
generous in death he was. I was touched. I set out to look
for you straight off. Every donkey I've met I've asked the
same question. And I've used up a life's supply of roses.
If you give me the nod I'll go and get you one. No?

LUCIUS: You will not believe what has happened to me!
Ah, Photis!

PHOTIS: Oh well. If you do happen to be Lucius, and you
ever get changed back, come and find me, my love.

Exit PHOTIS.

LUCIUS: It is as if she has set fire to me.
It hurts my heart – it is like memory.

Enter ISIS as the deck-chair lady and ice-cream woman.

ISIS: Ices! Ices! Excuse me.

LUCIUS makes no response.

I said excuse me.

No response.

Oi!

LUCIUS wakes up.

LUCIUS: What did you say?

ISIS: I said excuse me, ass. This beach is private.

LUCIUS: I'm so sorry, I'll move.

ISIS: Or else – I can hire you a patch.

LUCIUS: How much?

ISIS: The bit you're on is first class, you won't be able to afford that. But if you move over onto this stony place, we could probably come to an arrangement.

LUCIUS: Alright.

ISIS: How much have you got on you?

LUCIUS: Nothing. I'm an ass.

ISIS: Would you consider paying in kind?

LUCIUS: Like what?

ISIS: If you do children's rides in the afternoons, I'll let you sleep on this stony scrap at night, fair and square, no questions asked. Is it comfortable?

LUCIUS: No.

ISIS: Fine, I'm not overpaying you then. Is the deal done?

LUCIUS: And you will own me then?

ISIS: Oh no, oh no, it's just a temporary arrangement.

LUCIUS: But you will look after me – you won't let anyone else take me?

ISIS: If you do well I'll build you a shed at the month's end.

LUCIUS: Promise never to sell me!

ISIS: I can't sell what I don't own. You better get your head down, it'll be tomorrow soon.

LUCIUS: Alright. Thank you.

ISIS: See you later then.

She makes to leave.

LUCIUS: One moment –

ISIS: Yes?

LUCIUS: How can you understand what I'm saying?

She laughs.

Are you a goddess?

ISIS: What woman would say no to that question?

LUCIUS: Are you Minerva? Are you Juno? Are you the Mother of all things? Are you Venus?

ISIS: Oh! Look at that!

LUCIUS: Someone is drowning!

ISIS: Are you sure?

LUCIUS: I will swim out – she can cling to my back –

ISIS: I wouldn't do that. Look, she's fine now. Typical.

LUCIUS: Do you know her?

ISIS: That is Fortune, my daughter.

LUCIUS: Fortune? I hate her!

ISIS: She's just a baby!

LUCIUS: I did not know she was your daughter.

ISIS: Believe me, she does what I tell her.

LUCIUS: But who are you?

ISIS: You know these priests are always having strange dreams. They chant and they pray all day long and they stare and stare at the scriptures till their eyes catch light and set fire to their brains. These empty-headed old men, they've got so much room inside them, the stars and the moons, the whole universe can turn inside them, gods can come and go, so they do have strange dreams.

LUCIUS: What do they dream about?

ISIS: It will be busy here tomorrow. This whole beach will be crammed. You should stick around, you'll see some strange sights. A whole crowd of people will come singing, in wonderful costumes, and they will weave a ship out of reeds here on the sand and launch it onto the ocean, because now the year has come through its furious winter, roared itself quiet, stands in its cot blinking springtime and peace, and ships may sail again. You should stick around.

LUCIUS: What will happen then?

ISIS: Goddesses and gods, all dressed up, with their musical instruments, the priests in their white robes, the high priest with his sistrum wreathed with roses –

LUCIUS: With roses? Why?

ISIS: Because he has been told in a dream.

LUCIUS: These are the worshippers of Isis! You are Isis!

ISIS: Oh, look at Fortune!

LUCIUS: Riding on the back of a whale!

ISIS: Oops, it's dived!

LUCIUS: Why did you turn me into a donkey?

ISIS: The sky is also an animal, with its lion's head of
dawns and its peacock tail of stars. It prowls like a cat
round the world. Yes tomorrow will be a wonderful day
here on the beach. Loads to do and see. I do love a nice
day at the beach. With the donkeys.

Exit ISIS.

*Enter procession, comprised of all the characters from the story
of Cupid and Psyche and others who have been involved in
LUCIUS' journey, carrying a ship and headed by the high
PRIEST carrying roses.*

*LUCIUS wakes up and tries to get through the devotees to
the high priest, but is pushed away. He seems about to give
up, when the high PRIEST spots him and turns, and walks
towards him, holding out the roses. LUCIUS eats them and
turns back into a man.*

Expressions of amazement and astonishment.

LUCIUS: Do not beat me!

The people laugh.

LUCIUS sees statue of ISIS.

Aaaaaggghh! Aaaaaaagghhh! Get that woman away from
me! Hide her hair! It is like fire! I will kiss her and turn
back into a donkey! Cover my eyes, please, tie my
hands, chain me; stuff something into my mouth to stop
me speaking these words!

He tries to bray.

Tie rocks to my feet, hobble me! I am too beautiful, they will all want me!

PRIEST: Be calm – the goddess –

LUCIUS: Hide her! I will do something ugly!

PRIEST: It is Isis!

LUCIUS: Kill me now, kill me! Once I get a bad idea into my head there are no chains strong enough to stop me! The witch is watching me! I do not want to turn back! Kill me now, kill me! I will do bad things, these fingers are too clever – I am having wrong thoughts already – these lips – this quick tongue – perfect for lying. Will nobody buy me? Tie me to a mill, that would be best. I am a good donkey for robbers, you can cut open my belly, and what will you find inside me? Charite! I did not kill your citizens! Forgive me! Eheu cicatricum et sceleris pudet fratrumque – what language is that? I am an ass, I do not understand my own language! I will not do it! I will not do it!

PRIEST: Lucius, you have been released! The goddess
Has heard your prayer, she who is sometimes Venus,
Sometimes Athene, in some places Ceres
Or Hecate or Juno or Bellona,
But to the noble Ethiopians
And to the wise Egyptians who know better,
Isis – this goddess of all godesses
Has heard your plea for mercy, Lucius!
She loves you truly! You have been cast down
Lower than any man since the beginning,
Into the body of an animal,
But it is to the depths that heaven listens,
And so your cry was heard, and light came down
To clear your road – see how it now lies open!

The procession proceeds to the sea and launches the ship.

LUCIUS: And so I joined the procession, and the following
day I went to the temple of Isis and lay at her feet. then I
followed her into the temple and everyone else went
away but I just lay at her feet. And I worshipped her day
and night. And after a long time, and many dreams in
which the goddess spoke to me, telling me to be patient
and wait, at last the day came when I was to be admitted
to her secrets. And I ate no meat for ten days. And then I
was taken at night into her most sacred place in the
temple. And what happened there? I can't tell you that.
Well – but – I went down to hell, and I disintegrated – I
saw the sun shine at midnight – I saw the gods of light
and darkness, and I spoke to them. But you must not tell
this to anyone! Promise! Later the god Osiris in a dream
told me something that astonished me. That he wanted
me not to spend my days in a hushed place, praying, but
to enter the furious lawcourts and plead for those who
had lost all power, money, voice, state, status, species, as
once I did. So I took a boat to Rome, and I did what he
said. I had expected to be silent for the rest of my life.
But the god asked me to speak.

*LUCIUS is dressed in an Olympian robe and stands on a
stool, surrounded by everyone else.*

There is no hell, no matter how unknown,
She cannot lift us out of. With her arms
She holds apart the poles of what can happen,
She will not let them cause too wide a chasm,
Or crush the world into too tight a prison;
Her feet are on the sun and on the moon,
And with a kick she gives time its direction;
It is her wish that birds should fly, fish swim,
And people fall into the net of heaven.
Whatever I have done or heard or seen,
It was her speaking, she is her creation,

The very silence is her voice, wind blowing,
Lark filling up the emptiness of heaven.
What shall I do now she has set me free
From constant horror, hunger, rage and terror?
Now that her face has risen in my mind,
I am a sky whose sun does not go down.

PRIEST: Ploiaphesia!
Now let all ships depart and have fair sailing!

The boat is launched.

The End.